Right Here with You

Right Here with You

Mindfulness for Connection, Communication, and Deepening Our Relationships

Edited by Andrea Miller and the editors of *Lion's Roar*

SHAMBHALA

Shambhala Publications, Inc.
2129 13th Street
Boulder, Colorado 80302
www.shambhala.com

Cover art: Azuzl/iStock
Cover design: Amanda Weiss
Interior design: James D. Skatges

9 8 7 6 5 4 3 2 1

Printed in the United States of America

Shambhala Publications makes every effort to print on acid-free, recycled paper.
Shambhala Publications is distributed worldwide by Penguin Random House, Inc.,
and its subsidiaries.

Library of Congress Cataloging-in-Publication Data
Names: Miller, Andrea (Shambhala sun editor)
Title: Right here with you: mindfulness for connection, communication, and
deepening our relationships / edited by Andrea Miller and the editors of Lion's Roar.
Description: Boulder, Colorado: Shambhala, 2025. | Originally published by
Shambhala in 2011. | Includes bibliographical references.
Identifiers: LCCN 2024022274 | ISBN 9781590309049 (pbk.: alk. paper) |
ISBN 9781645473121 (pbk.: 2025 ed.)
Subjects: LCSH: Interpersonal relations. | Love—Religious aspects—Buddhism. |
Interpersonal relations—Religious aspects—Buddhism.
Classification: LCC BF575.L8 R54 2025 | DDC 294.3/5677—dc23/eng/20240603
LC record available at https://lccn.loc.gov/2024022274

Contents

Editor's Introduction   ix

PART ONE: Visions of Mindful Loving

LOVE IS BEING PRESENT   3
Thich Nhat Hanh

SAYING YES TO AN OPEN HEART   12
Diana Winston

THE GREAT MIRROR OF RELATIONSHIP   15
Dzogchen Ponlop

GOING BEYOND DISAPPOINTMENT   18
Judith Simmer-Brown

FALLING IN LOVE   23
Norman Fischer

PART TWO: Preparing the Ground

MAKING FRIENDS WITH OURSELVES   31
Moh Hardin

RECOGNIZING OUR BASIC GOODNESS   41
Tara Brach

CHOOSING A PARTNER   50
David Richo

NO GAIN   57
Barry Magid

PART THREE: Being in Relationship

MARRIAGE ON A PLATE   63
Karen Maezen Miller

MOVING TARGET   69
Erik Hansen

TO LOVE AND BE LOVED   72
Rabbi Harold Kushner

FINDING FORGIVENESS IN A ZIPLOC   77
Jane Hamilton

BECOMING INTIMATE WITH FEAR   82
Ezra Bayda

MEMOIR OF AN UNLIKELY MARRIAGE   92
Ellen Graf

PRESENT MOMENT LISTENING   100
Arthur Jeon

PART FOUR: Dealing with Difficulties

THOSE AREN'T FIGHTING WORDS, DEAR   105
Laura Munson

IT USED TO BE SO EXCITING   110
Brenda Shoshanna

THE HIDDEN TREASURE OF ANGER   114
Polly Young-Eisendrath

THE GREEN-EYED MONSTER   119
Geri Larkin

MY MARITAL STATUS   124
James Kullander

PART FIVE: Growing Apart

MAKING FRIENDS WITH HEARTBREAK   137
Susan Piver

OF COURSE I'M ANGRY   142
Gabriel Cohen

I THINK WE SHOULD STOP SEEING EACH OTHER   150
Karen Kissel Wegela

WHEN RELATIONSHIPS END   154
David Richo

LET IT BEE   161
Jennifer Lauck

PART SIX: Love as a Spiritual Path

INTIMATE RELATIONSHIP AS A SPIRITUAL CRUCIBLE   169
John Welwood

MARRIAGE AS A PATH OF COMPASSION   180
Richard Borofsky

MAY ALL BEINGS BE HAPPY   186
Joseph Goldstein

THAT'S THE POWER OF LOVE   190
The Fourteenth Dalai Lama

SEARCHING FOR THE HEART OF COMPASSION   194
Marc Ian Barasch

My Vows   205
Susan Piver

Contributors   211
Credits   217

Editor's Introduction

Where I come from there are six months of icy, gray winter. There are sea chanteys and the introspective wail of bagpipes. And there is fish-and-chips—salty with a splash of vinegar. In contrast, where my husband, Adán, comes from there are magenta bougainvilleas, bright green banana leaves, turquoise rivers. The flavor is spice tucked into corn, and the beats are quick—cumbia, merengue, salsa.

Our cultural mix is exciting; we're two worlds meeting and making something fresh. Our language is our own intimate *Spanglish,* vocabularies from two dictionaries giving us all the more words for love, for celebration. With flowers and photos, we build an altar for the Day of the Dead, then March 17 comes along, and we get decked out in green. For both holidays, however, we skip the beer, the two of us in perfect agreement that it's almost never the right drink.

But don't let me mislead you; sometimes our relationship is not two worlds meeting; it's two worlds colliding. We misunderstand each other, get confused, hurt, angry. And frequently it takes a good long time to unravel the threads and figure out the linguistic twist or cultural assumption that caused the problem. When you grow up in a particular culture, certain things are so obvious, so taken for granted, that you'd never think to explain them; you don't even think about them. Then you meet someone and you move in with them, and those obvious things are not always obvious to that person. When you realize this, you are dumbfounded, and so is your partner.

But marrying someone with a passport from the same country as you does not entirely prevent the aforementioned scenario from unfolding.

Even if you and your partner grew up on the same street, you will occasionally feel a culture clash. Some people say it's because men are from Mars and women are from Venus, but I doubt that; the gay and lesbian couples I know also have profound misunderstandings that bear an uncanny resemblance to the misunderstandings of heterosexual couples. It seems to me that each human being is a culture unto themself. When there is chemistry between two people, lots can grow: passion, joy, friendship, commitment, but so can misunderstandings, mounting anger, crushing disappointment.

For better, for worse, and for all the moments in between, my hope is that *Right Here with You* can offer some perspective. I know that, because of the pieces in this anthology, I've gained a greater understanding of what it means to be intimate and how mindfulness can deepen connection. But—word of warning—none of the contributing authors offers a quick, easy path to finding perfect love. Rather, they offer something more realistic and ultimately, I believe, more satisfying: a mindful approach to relationships that takes practice and time.

Mindfulness is a word many people kick around these days, so much so that in some circles the meaning of it may be watered down and confused—somehow equated with "not being spacey." But what is mindfulness really? It is paying close yet gentle attention to whatever life brings and allowing our awareness to make us more compassionate and loving.

The Buddha practiced and taught mindfulness; yet it doesn't belong to any one religion. Christians, Jews, Hindus, Muslims, atheists—all can bring the practice into their lives. Indeed, a secular mindfulness movement is gaining momentum. Mindfulness, free of religious trappings, is now giving a more humane face to health care, education, law enforcement, business, and domestic life.

Right Here with You: Bringing Mindful Awareness into Our Relationships is divided into six sections. Part 1, "Visions of Mindful Loving," is an exploration of what we might aim for in our relationships. This section seeks to answer the questions: what does mindful love look like and feel like, and what are its qualities? It begins with a simple yet profound teaching by the renowned Zen monk Thich Nhat Hanh. Mindful love is the only true kind, he tells us, because our sincere presence is the most precious gift we can give. But how can we truly be present for those we love? Thich Nhat Hanh offers a variety of practical tools to set us on the path.

"The Great Mirror of Relationship," by the Tibetan meditation master Dzogchen Ponlop, points out that none of us is independent; we all need others. Yet mindful love is not needy. A healthy intimate relationship is like two rings coming together, overlapping just in the middle. There's a common space in the center containing mutual joy and responsibility; nonetheless, there are also the two sides that allow room for individuality.

Part 2, "Preparing the Ground," explores the notion that if we want to create mindful relationships, we must start by working on our relationship with ourselves. As meditation instructor Moh Hardin explains, the foundation of love for others is unconditional friendship toward oneself. Psychologist Tara Brach further explores self-love by telling the story of one of her clients, a woman who doesn't know if she is more angry with her husband for cheating or with herself for potentially driving him to do so.

In "Choosing a Partner," psychologist David Richo explains how we can bring greater awareness to the process of looking for and embarking on a new relationship. Zen teacher Barry Magid cautions us, however, against expecting relationships to solve all of our problems. Our lover cannot save us from life's inevitable ups and downs. Indeed, to the contrary, our partner will certainly challenge us, press our buttons—and that's the good news.

Part 3 of *Right Here with You* is "Being in Relationship." This section is about the experience of living together day in and day out, so what could be more appropriate than kicking it off with "Marriage on a Plate" by Zen teacher Karen Maezen Miller, which is about the daily grind of domestic chores and how they can either wear away your relationship or transform it into something deeper.

Rabbi Harold Kushner and novelist Jane Hamilton both write about forgiveness in relationships. Kushner's take on the topic is that couples need to let go of who's right and who's wrong. They need to be like children who squabble but then quickly let go of their hard feelings so they can resume playing together. Hamilton is also on board for opening the heart and forgiving quickly. As she tells us in her piece, it was in an airport that she had an epiphany: forgiveness is easy when you understand that there is no separation between you and the person who's getting on your last nerve.

Part 4, "Dealing with Difficulties," offers mindful responses to the common conflicts and problems that arise in relationships. "It Used to Be

So Exciting," by psychologist Brenda Shoshanna, focuses on the problem of boredom and the importance of learning to sit still with this uncomfortable feeling, even when it tells you to run away. After all, if we're constantly in pursuit of newness, how will we come to appreciate the beauty of ordinary routines? Zen teacher Geri Larkin's piece deals with jealousy and how mindfulness can help us to look more deeply and honestly at this troublesome emotion so we can finally find freedom from it. A critical thing to remember when we have problems is the fleeting nature of life. Take James Kullander in "My Marital Status." When the woman he loves becomes ill, they must face the ultimate difficulty.

Part 5 is "Growing Apart," and the first two essays are a study in contrast. The respective authors are Susan Piver and Gabriel Cohen, and they were both on the receiving end of a breakup. Piver's reaction was to melt in tears and have trouble getting out of bed. Her piece explores how to be gentle and patient with yourself during a breakup. Cohen, however, reacted to his divorce with fury, and he examines the pointlessness of anger. He can stew all day about his ex-wife but discovers that the only person who's hurt by this stewing is himself.

The final section of the book is titled "Love as a Spiritual Path." Here, we learn that, ultimately, love can be seen as a journey that awakens the best in human nature—loving-kindness, understanding, compassion, and fearlessness. In "Intimate Relationship as a Spiritual Crucible" by John Welwood, we see the commonalities between intimate relationships and spiritual training. Meanwhile, "May All Beings Be Happy" by Joseph Goldstein and "That's the Power of Love" by the Dalai Lama describe ways of taking the love we feel for our partners or our families and expanding it to embrace all beings.

Love all beings, or love even one? This is the question Susan Piver grapples with in "My Vows," the last piece in this collection. Ultimately, Piver chooses both—to love and commit to both her fiancé and to the wider world. My hope is that that's the kind of choice we all make.

Publishing *Right Here with You* has involved the effort and support of many people. I would like to thank Eden Steinberg, my editor at Shambhala Publications, and my colleagues at *Shambhala Sun* (now *Lion's Roar*) and *Buddhadharma*, in particular Melvin McLeod, Barry Boyce, Andy Karr, and Jessica von Handorf.

On a personal note, many thanks to my husband for his help, patience, and love. Many thanks also to my mother, Alanna, whose pithy gems of relationship advice will stay with me all my life, and to my fathers, Stephen and Mark, who taught me the value of the written word.

Andrea Miller
Editor
Lion's Roar

PART ONE

Visions of Mindful Loving

Love Is Being Present

Thich Nhat Hanh

The Zen monk and Nobel Prize nominee Thich Nhat Hanh is one of the world's leading teachers of mindfulness. Here, he explains that mindfulness lies at the very heart of true love.

TO LOVE IS, above all, to be there. But being there is not an easy thing. Some training is necessary, some practice. If you are not there, how can you love? Being there is very much an art, the art of meditation, because meditating is bringing your true presence to the here and now. The question that arises is, do you have time to love?

I know a boy of twelve whose father asked him one day, "Son, what would you like for your birthday present?" The boy did not know how to answer his father, who was a very rich man, able to buy anything for his son. But the boy did not want anything except his father's presence. Because the role the father played kept him very busy, he did not have time to devote to his wife and children. Being rich is an obstacle to loving. When you are rich, you want to continue to be rich, and so you end up devoting all your time, all your energy in your daily life, to staying rich. If this father were to understand what true love is, he would do whatever was necessary to find time for his son and his wife.

The most precious gift you can give to the one you love is your true presence. What must you do to really be there? Those who have practiced Buddhist meditation know that meditating is, above all, being present—to yourself, to those you love, to life.

So I would propose a very simple practice to you, the practice of mindful breathing: "I breathe in—I know that I am breathing in; I breathe out—I know that I am breathing out." If you do that with a little concentration, then you will be able to really be there, because in daily life our mind and our body are rarely together. Our body might be there, but our mind is somewhere else. Maybe you are lost in regrets about the past, maybe in worries about the future, or else you are preoccupied with your plans, with anger or with jealousy. And so your mind is not really there with your body.

Between the mind and the body, there is something that can serve as a bridge. The moment you begin to practice mindful breathing, your body and your mind begin to come together with one another. It takes only ten to twenty seconds to accomplish this miracle called oneness of body and mind. With mindful breathing, you can bring body and mind together in the present moment, and every one of us can do it, even a child.

If the father I was talking about had known that, he would have begun to breathe in and breathe out mindfully, and then one or two minutes later, he would have approached his son, he would have looked at him with a smile, and he would have said this: "My dear, I am here for you." This is the greatest gift you can give to someone you love.

BEING RIGHT HERE

In Buddhism, we talk about mantras. A mantra is a powerful statement that, once it is uttered, can entirely change a situation, our mind, our body, or a person. But this statement must be spoken in a state of concentration, that is to say, a state in which body and mind are absolutely in a state of unity. What you say then, in this state of being, becomes a mantra.

So I am going to present to you a very effective mantra: "Dear one, I am here for you." Perhaps this evening you will try for a few minutes to practice mindful breathing in order to bring your body and mind together. You will approach the person you love, and with this mindfulness, with this concentration, you will look into his or her eyes, and you will begin to utter this formula: "Dear one, I am really here for you." You must say that with your body and with your mind at the same time, and then you will see the transformation.

Do you have enough time to love? Can you make sure that in your everyday life you have a little time to love? We do not have much time together; we are too busy. In the morning while eating breakfast, we do not look at the person we love, we do not have enough time for it. We eat very quickly while thinking about other things, and sometimes we even hold a newspaper that hides the face of the person we love. In the evening when we come home, we are too tired to be able to look at the person we love.

We must bring about a revolution in our way of living our everyday lives, because our happiness, our lives, are within ourselves.

RECOGNIZING THE PRESENCE OF THE OTHER

I would now like to present a second mantra to you. When you are really there, you have the ability to recognize the presence of the other. To be there is the first step, and recognizing the presence of the other is the second step. To love is to be; to be loved is to be recognized by the other. If you love someone and you continue to ignore his or her presence, this is not true love. Perhaps your intention is not to ignore this person, but the way you act, look, and speak does not manifest the desire to recognize the presence of the other. When we are loved, we wish the other to recognize our presence, and this is a very important practice. You must do whatever is necessary to be able to do this: recognize the presence of the person you love several times each day.

To attain this goal, it is also necessary to practice oneness of body and mind. Practice mindful breathing three times, five times, seven times; then you approach this person, you look at him or her mindfully, with a smile, and you begin to say the second mantra: "Dear one, I know that you are here, and I am very glad about it." If you practice in this way, with a lot of concentration and mindfulness, you will see that this person will open immediately, like a flower blossoming. To be loved is to be recognized, and you can do that several times a day. It is not difficult at all, and it is a true meditation.

Whatever you do mindfully is meditation. When you touch a flower, you can touch it with your fingers, but better yet, you can touch it mindfully, with your full awareness. "I am breathing in—I know that the flower is there; I am breathing out—I smile at the flower." While you are practicing in this way, you are really there, and at the same time, the flower is really there. If you are not really there, nothing is there. The sunset is something marvelous and so is the full moon, but since you are not really there, the sunset is not for you. From time to time, I let myself look at the full moon; I take a deep breath in and a deep breath out, and I practice: "I know you are there, and I am very glad about it." I practice that with the full moon, with the cherry blossoms. . . . We are surrounded by miracles, but we have to recognize them; otherwise there is no life.

The Buddha told us this: "The past is no longer there, the future is not here yet; there is only one moment in which life is available, and that is the present moment." To meditate is to bring body and mind back to the present moment so that you do not miss your appointment with life.

In Albert Camus's novel *The Stranger,* a man named Meursault is condemned to death. Three days before his execution, he is in his cell, looking at the ceiling, and he discovers a square of blue sky appearing through the skylight. He is able for the first time in his life to touch the blue sky. At forty years of age, strangely enough, this man is seeing the sun for the first time. Of course, he had looked at the blue sky and the stars more than once before, but this time it was for real. We might not know how to touch the blue sky in such a profound way. The moment of awareness Camus describes is mindfulness: suddenly you are able to touch life.

In Buddhism, the energy that helps us to touch life deeply is called *smrti,* the energy of mindfulness. Everyone possesses a seed of this energy. If we practice touching deeply, if we practice breathing deeply, we can generate this energy.

When you breathe in, you recognize at that moment that this is an in-breath; when you breathe out, you are aware of the fact that this is an out-breath. Recognizing what is there in the present moment is attention. That is the energy of mindfulness. So then, with this mantra, you are going to practice recognizing the presence of the person you love: "Dear one, I know that you are there, and I am very glad about it."

This is real meditation. In this particular meditation, all at once there is love, compassion, joy, and freedom—the four constituents of true love.

Being There When Someone Is Suffering

The third mantra is used in circumstances in which the person you love is suffering. When you are living mindfully, you know what is happening in your situation in the present moment. Therefore, it is easy for you to notice when the person you love is suffering. At such a time, you go to him or her, with your body and mind unified, with concentration, and you utter the third mantra: "Dear one, I know that you are suffering; that is why I am here for you."

When we are suffering, we have a strong need for the presence of the person we love. If we are suffering and the man or woman we love ignores us, then we suffer more. So what we can do—and right away—is to manifest our true presence to the beloved person and say the mantra with force: "Dear one, I know that you are suffering; that is why I am here for you." Even before you actually do something to help, the person you love is relieved. Your presence is a miracle, your understanding of his or her pain is a miracle, and you are able to offer this aspect of your love immediately.

Really try to be there—for yourself, for life, for the people that you love. Recognize the presence of those who live in the same place as you and try to be there when one of them is suffering, because your presence is so precious for this person. In this way, you will be practicing love twenty-four hours a day.

OVERCOMING PRIDE

The fourth mantra is more difficult to practice. It has to do with a situation in which you are suffering yourself and you think that your suffering has been created by the person you love most in the world. If it had been someone else who had said that to you or done that to you, without a doubt you would be suffering less. But in this case, it is the person you love most in the world who said that to you, who did that to you, and you are suffering more. You are deeply hurt by the fact that your suffering was caused by the person you love the most. You feel like going to your room, closing the door, staying by yourself, and crying. You refuse to go to him or her to ask for help. So now it is pride that is the obstacle.

According to the teaching of the Buddha, in true love, there is no place for pride. If you are suffering, every time you are suffering, you must go to the person in question and ask for his or her help. That is true love. Do not let pride keep you apart. If you think your love for this person is true love, you must overcome your pride; you must always go to him or her. That is why I have invented this mantra for you. Practice so as to bring about oneness of your body and mind before going to the person to say the fourth mantra: "Dear one, I am suffering. Help me, please." This is very simple but very hard to do.

I would like to tell you a story from my country. A young man went off to war, leaving his pregnant wife behind. Two years later, he was able to return home, and the young woman went with their young son to meet her husband. They cried together out of joy. In Vietnam, in our tradition, when an event of this kind takes place, it has to be announced to the ancestors. So the young father asked his wife to go to the market to buy the things that are needed for the offering that is placed on the altar to the ancestors. Such an altar is found in every house. Each morning we burn a stick of incense to our ancestors on this altar, and in this way, we make a connection with them. Burning this incense, adorning the altar with photographs of our ancestors, and dusting the shrine off are very important gestures. These are moments in which we come in contact with our ancestors. There are people living in the world who are completely uprooted because they do not practice such a turning toward their ancestors.

So the young wife went off to the market. During this time, the young father was trying to convince his child to call him Daddy. The little boy refused: "Mister, you're not my daddy. My daddy is somebody else. He visits us every night, and my mommy talks to him every night, and very often she cries with him. And every time my mommy sits down, he sits down too. Every time she lies down, he lies down too." After he heard these words, the young father's happiness entirely evaporated. His heart turned into a block of ice. He felt hurt, deeply humiliated, and that is why, when his wife came home, he would no longer look at her or speak a word to her. He ignored her. The woman herself began to suffer; she felt humiliated, hurt. When the offering was placed on the altar, the young father burned the incense, recited the prayers to the ancestors, and did the four traditional prostrations. Then he picked the mat up instead of leaving it there for his wife so she could do the four prostrations in her turn. In his mind, he thought that she was not qualified to present herself before the ancestors, and she was humiliated by this.

After the ceremony, he didn't stay at the house to eat but went to the village and spent the day in a bar. He tried to forget his suffering by drinking alcohol, and he did not come back to the house until very late at night.

The following day, it was the same thing, and this went on for several days in a row. The young woman could not take it anymore. Her suffering was so great that, in the end, she threw herself in the river and drowned.

When the young father heard this news, he returned to the house, and that night he was the one who went to get the lamp and lit it. Suddenly the child cried out, "Mister, Mister, it's my daddy, he's come back!" And he pointed to the shadow of his father on the wall. "You know, Mister, my father comes every night. Mommy talks to him and sometimes she cries; and every time she sits down, my daddy sits down too." In reality, this woman had been alone in the house too much, and every night she had talked to her shadow: "My dear one, you are so far away from me. How can I raise my child all by myself? . . . You must come back home soon." She would cry, and, of course, every time she sat down, the shadow would also sit down. Now the husband's false perception was no longer there, but it was too late—his wife was already dead.

A false perception is something that can destroy an entire family. The Buddha told us a number of times that we are subject to false perceptions in our everyday life. Therefore we have to pay close attention to our perceptions. There are people who hang on to their false perceptions for ten or twenty years, and during this time they continue to suffer and make other people suffer.

Why did the young father not want to talk this thing over with his wife? Because pride got between them. If he had asked his wife, "Who is this person who came every night? Our child told me about him. I am suffering so much, my darling, you have to help me. Explain to me who this person is." If he had done that, his wife would have had a chance to explain, and the drama could have been avoided. However, it was not only his fault, but that of his young wife as well. She could have come to him and asked him the reason for his change in attitude: "Husband, why don't you look at me anymore? Why don't you talk to me? Have I done something awful that I deserve such treatment? I am suffering so much, dear husband, you have to help me."

She did not do this, and I do not want you to make the same mistake in your everyday life. We are subject to false perceptions every day, so we have to pay attention. Every time you think it is somebody else who is causing the suffering, you must remember this story. You must always check things out by going to the person in question and asking for his or her help: "Dear one, I am suffering so much. Help me, please."

THE FOUR ASPECTS OF LOVE

According to the Buddhist tradition, there are four elements of true love. The first is *maitri,* which can be translated as loving-kindness or benevolence. Loving-kindness is not only the desire to make someone happy, to bring joy to a beloved person; it is the *ability* to bring joy and happiness to the person you love, because even if your intention is to love this person, your love might make him or her suffer.

Training is needed in order to love properly; and to be able to give happiness and joy, you must practice *deep looking* directed toward the person you love. Because if you do not understand this person, you cannot love properly. Understanding is the essence of love. If you cannot understand, you cannot love. That is the message of the Buddha. If a husband, for example, does not understand his wife's deepest troubles, her deepest aspirations, if he does not understand her suffering, he will not be able to love her in the right way. Without understanding, love is an impossible thing.

What must we do in order to understand a person? We must have time; we must practice deep looking directed toward this person. We must be there, attentive; we must observe, we must look. And the fruit of this deep looking is called understanding. Love is a true thing if it is made up of a substance called understanding.

The second element of true love is compassion, *karuna.* This is not only the desire to ease the pain of another person but the *ability* to do so. You must practice deep looking in order to gain a good understanding of the nature of the suffering of this person, in order to be able to help him or her to change. Knowledge and understanding are always at the root of the practice. The practice of understanding is the practice of meditation. To meditate is to look deeply into the heart of things.

The third element of true love is joy, *mudita.* If there is no joy in love, it is not true love. If you are suffering all the time, if you cry all the time, and if you make the person you love cry, this is not really love—it is even the opposite. If there is no joy in your love, you can be sure that it is not true love.

The fourth element is *upeksha,* equanimity or freedom. In true love, you attain freedom. When you love, you bring freedom to the person you love. If the opposite is true, it is not true love. You must love in such a way that the person you love feels free, not only outside but also inside. "Dear one, do you have enough space in your heart and all around you?" This is an intelligent question for testing out whether your love is something real.

Saying Yes to an Open Heart

Diana Winston

If you continually open and attend to your experiences, then over time, the mindfully opened heart is more and more just who you are. Here, nationally known mindfulness teacher Diana Winston shares her discovery of love's connection to the present moment.

I'D LIKE TO PROPOSE that mindfulness—true-blue mindfulness—*is* the open heart. Sure, the purists can define mindfulness as "paying attention to the present moment with an open and curious stance," but that definition can be staid, sort of dull, and it can inadvertently take the heart out of a practice, which is, in truth, all heart.

I remember in my early years of mindfulness practice I got attached to subtle mental states of concentration. I was intensely curious and amazed by my mind, but secretly I felt the practice was a little dry—too much in the head. So I spent a few years seeking out gurus in India, hoping for a devotional hit to make my practice juicier. I later realized I was looking for love in all the wrong places—outside myself instead of inside.

That's when I discovered that mindfulness practice itself is the open heart. And here's how it works: First you start out on the cushion (or chair for the less pretzelly inclined), and you attend to your present moment experience, no matter what it is—good, bad, or ugly. And as you practice and get some skill—*Hey, I can sit here and be okay in the midst of knee pain, in the midst of my aching back, my frayed nerves*—then you realize just this: the capacity to be mindful means having an open heart. It's not a theory, it's a heart/body-felt insight.

Why is this so? Because as you sit there, hour after hour, you learn to say yes. Yes to your jagged breathing, yes to your itchy scalp. Yes to the leaf-blower dude across the street, yes to your grief and pain and shame and grandiosity and fear. Not because you want to act on these things, but because they're true and fleeting and simply part of who you are (but not the half of who you really are). Your nervous system begins to relax—at last you're acknowledging the truth of things.

Saying yes means attending to and surrendering to your experience, whatever it is. It means feeling your body when you're in the midst of a strong reaction or emotion and letting whatever you find be there. It means coming back to your breath again and again. It means noticing that thoughts and feelings and sensations come and go.

You say yes to your pride, your stupidity, your murderous rage. Naturally you don't act on your murderous rage, but you allow it to be true within you. It is a very inclusive practice. Nothing is ever left out.

You discover that if you are pushing away your experience, even ever so slightly, your mindfulness is not fully realized, not quite formed. It is tainted by aversion, even just subtly. Now sometimes you truly can't say yes, and then you say yes to the no: *I hate that I'm not feeling okay, but I'm actually okay with not being okay.*

Saying yes in mindfulness practice eventually begins to spill over into your everyday experience. You start to say yes—with awareness—again and again: yes when that guy cuts you off in traffic; yes when your e-mail box is spammed to the brim; yes when your doctor is an hour late; yes even when you lose a treasured person, place, or thing. You say yes to your experience of the present moment, whatever it is. You no longer reject and armor your heart. Not that you necessarily agree with the moment or would wish it on anyone or think it's desirable or wouldn't try to rectify injustice, but you say yes because whatever life brings is just that, life as it is. And by saying yes, you let go deep down inside and can step forward with poise and balance and clarity to the next right thing.

My six-month-old daughter has been waking me up hourly to night-nurse. Sometimes I say no. *Oh god, not again. What's wrong with her? Will*

I ever get to sleep again? In those moments, mindfulness is a vague "good idea" somewhere in my sleep-deprived brain. But other nights when she cries, I simply, without thought, say yes. *Yes, darling, feast. Yes, I'll be with you. Yes, I'm awake, and that's just how things are.* I listen to the stillness of the night (rare in Los Angeles), feel her warm body and attend to her snuffling slurps, and sigh that yes, this is life. A deep peace sets in over me.

By doing this practice of yes, by mindfully embracing each moment with a willingness to accept things as they are, with a willingness to be with life—inner and outer—exactly as it unfolds, you may be able to look down at your chest and realize that your heart is gigantic. It's expansive, spacious, broken open, like a big, fat suitcase overflowing with warm, comfy, oh-so-familiar clothes.

You open and open, you attend and attend, you say yes again and again, and then over time, the mindfully opened heart is more and more just who you are.

The Great Mirror of Relationship

DZOGCHEN PONLOP

Relationship is a mirror in which we can see ourselves, and that mirror can be so very clear. In it, says Tibetan Buddhist teacher and scholar Dzogchen Ponlop, we discover our tendencies, our weaknesses, and our strengths. We discover who we really are.

WE CANNOT EXIST without depending on others. When I go to the grocery store and buy an apple, I might feel very independent. I walk in, grab an apple, pay with my own money, and go home and eat by myself. But, in fact, I can only enjoy this apple because it is connected to so many people and conditions: the store owner, the shelf stockers, the truckers, the farmers, all the way back to the seed and the earth. There's so much connection all the time.

Of all the relationships we have in this interdependent experience of ours, the most direct, most emotional, and most apt to bring great joy and suffering is a close, intimate relationship with another human being. We give it great, special prominence in our mind, but it helps to remember that it is the same as the apple. It's about interconnection, interdependence.

From a Buddhist point of view, relationship is a great mirror. It is the mirror in which we see ourselves, in which we discover ourselves. That mirror can be distorted. I remember the first time I saw myself in a funhouse mirror: "Oh, what happened to me? I'm all stretched out." The mirror can also be very clear. We can see ourselves and what we are up to so directly. That makes relationship a beautiful experience.

When we sit by ourselves, it's easy to enjoy our mental games, fantasies, ego trips, and so forth. We can go on and on and on without any problem. But try that with your partner! Then here comes the mirror. The mirror will reflect and show you your ugly ego trips. A mirror is very neutral—it just reflects. It doesn't take any sides. It is just a mirror for both of us.

In this mirror, we discover ourselves—our tendencies, our weaknesses, and our strengths. We discover our good qualities as well as our negative qualities. So this mirror becomes a very precious teacher for us, a very precious path. The mirror of relationship becomes a very precious teaching for us to discover who we really are and where we are on the path and in the world altogether.

This is a lot to take in, so our tendency is to see what we want to see in this relationship mirror. The problem with this approach in a close relationship is that two people are seeing two different things. If I want to see something and she wants to see something else, we're both seeing two different things. As a result, we're being thrown off from the balance, the benefit, the preciousness of the relationship, the mirror. We would rather idealize our relationship; we would rather escape. We would rather live in the future than in this very immediate present moment. But if we can practice being in this present moment, relationship can become a path, and the mirror can be a great teacher.

In our relationship with another, we often misunderstand how we are connected. We may think we are two made into one, or we may think we are completely independent. My father taught me that a marriage or partnership, an intimate relationship with another human being, is like two rings coming together. You can illustrate it with your fingers. Make a ring with each hand, then join the rings together. There's a common space in the center. There is mutual responsibility, joy, and sharing, yet at the same time, we must understand there are also the two sides. There is not only the middle; individual space is also necessary.

If we try to overlap these two rings totally, we lose balance. There is a common bond, but there are also two individual mind streams. We must respect that and allow the other independence. The common space respects the individual space. We cannot overpower the other or make them just like us. The other not only has needs but also individual, habitual karmic habits that you cannot change. They need to initiate change themselves; you cannot forcibly change them. Buddhism teaches us that you cannot change someone's karma; not even Buddha can do that. He said, "I can only show you the path; to do it is totally up to you."

That's the basic principle in a relationship—we share. We share our wisdom, our knowledge; we allow ourselves to be a mirror, but it's up to the individual to make the choice. We must respect that. We must know that the other acts out of habit pattern, just as we do. Just as we cannot be forcibly changed from the outside, so too with them.

Problems begin when we lose the balance that comes from understanding the interplay of connection and separateness. We lose the sense of mindfulness when we lose the basic balance of the selfless, egoless teaching and become selfish, ego-centered, or even egomaniacal.

That's where *dukkha* (suffering) begins and joy ends, where the joy of relationship ends and the dukkha of relationship begins. When a relationship is troubling, that will stimulate our path. We can't expect it to always be perfect. In the mirror of relationship, we discover all these things. We discover the real nature of relationship, and we discover how we go off balance, how we lose the egoless, selfless view, how we lose the sense of love and caring.

Practicing mindfulness and awareness can help us see in the mirror more clearly. Mindfulness can tame the mental wildness that causes us to go so off balance. Mindfulness puts that wild mind in a corral. Once the wild horse of our mind is a little settled, we can train it by tying it to the post of awareness. Then we can train the horse to do all sorts of things, including to exert itself on the path of relationship and take joy and delight in loving.

Going Beyond Disappointment

Judith Simmer-Brown

Judith Simmer-Brown, who leads workshops on how meditation can help us create more fulfilling and lasting relationships, says that it is only when the romance bubble pops that true love begins. It's in disappointment, she says, that we can find an appreciation for who our partner is—beyond fantasy.

ROMANTIC LOVE HAS BECOME a kind of religion in Western culture. In his landmark book, *Love in the Western World,* Denis de Rougemont traced the development of romantic love in the courtly tradition of the Middle Ages, describing it as a Christian heresy. He described how Christian nobles transferred their devotion from the unattainable God to the unattainable lover, imbuing her with ideal traits beyond those of any mortal woman. He argued that such a view of romantic love survives today; even now, one of the most pervasive and unacknowledged forms of theism is our romantic life. We have made the lover into a god, and we are in love with love rather than with the lover. The lover is cast in a specific role in order for him or her to remain a god.

What are the qualities of romantic relationships? First of all, romantic love thrives on separation. The unattainable love is the most attractive one—someone who is married to someone else, living in a distant city, or in a nexus of the forbidden. The girl or boy next door is not a good candidate for romantic fantasy, and neither is one's spouse. Separation makes the heart grow fonder and more passionate, because with separation, the fantasy of the lover can be kept alive. The reality of the person cannot threaten the fantasy. For this reason, many newlyweds become quickly disillusioned over the mundane realities of married life. The courtship was so exciting, but marriage is too real, too ordinary.

Because romance thrives on separation, it is sexy but never sexually fulfilled. If one were truly satiated sexually, then the romance would be threatened. Often, the lover chooses the mystical option of desire, giving up the living, breathing sexual partner for the fantasy of the unattainable lover. Illicit love affairs are hot but are rarely resolved in marriage.

Secondly, romantic love is frightfully impersonal. We are looking for our "type"—an intellectual, a jock, an ethereal blonde. Our typing can become very subtle, including our lover's taste in clothes or way of walking. But we are in love with a fantasy; the person of the lover is absent. It actually helps not to have the person around too much, because they might destroy the fantasy. We have a terror that love may become too real.

Making the lover into a god, we foster a sense of poverty in ourselves. This is a lack of completion, which manifests as insatiable desire. We feel inadequate and helpless without a lover. When we have made the lover into a god, we can never join our lover. We are stuck in a situation of desperate longing, of neediness and insecurity. This is why de Rougemont called romantic love a Christian heresy; passion means suffering, and we have misplaced our devotion onto a fantasy that has trapped us forever in unhappiness.

There is a death wish at the heart of romantic love. In classical myths and literature, one possesses the lover completely only in death—and we see this played out daily in newspaper accounts of domestic disputes. The desire for union with the lover is desire for oblivion, and anything more pedestrian interferes with the fantasy.

This is the most difficult trait to acknowledge: romantic love glorifies unhappiness. The pain of romantic passion is something we find delicious. This is clear in our entertainments—films, novels, television, ballet, opera, and plays. We entertain ourselves with the scrumptious pain of a romantic story, and that pain makes us feel so alive, so real, and so convinced of the meaningfulness of romantic love.

When we examine this carefully, we sense the unhealthiness of a cult that glorifies unhappiness. So what choice do we have? We realize how unhappy romantic love is, but what else is there? All of us have experienced the way the bubble pops in romantic relationships, and the ensuing disappointment and disillusionment. We say we have fallen out of love. We begin to feel the pointlessness of the fantasy, and we see the lover as a stranger or even an enemy. We feel so lonely and hurt.

But disappointment is simply the flip side of romantic love. In both cases, we are so totally wrapped up with our own fantasy that we never really see the other person. We don't see the person we're in love with; we don't see the person we're breaking up with. Both situations are impersonal.

Disappointment is the more fruitful side of the coin because it occurs when our ambition and fantasy about the relationship become bankrupt. Disappointment could be the beginning of a true relationship. There is a kind of loss of innocence in disappointment that can lead to the appreciation of the lover for who he or she is—beyond fantasy.

Staying with disappointment requires a certain amount of bravery, for we find ourselves alone. Often, it has been our fear of loneliness that caused us to so earnestly seek out a relationship; we need someone, anyone, to make us feel secure, solid, alive. And here we are again, alone and desolate.

Because this is such a familiar feeling, we begin to see that no one can take away our fear of loneliness. Our aloneness will always come up; even the best relationships end through death or change. When we treasure our aloneness, it becomes so refreshing. When we feel it and acknowledge it as the basis of all our relationships, there is tremendous freedom. Of course, this guarantees nothing about the relationship itself.

When aloneness and disappointment dawn for us, the relationship might have the space to begin. There is tremendous groundlessness, for we really don't know where the relationship is going. There may be good times, there may be bad times. What happens, though, is that we begin to have a relationship with a person. We can begin to see the lover as someone separate from us, and we feel aloneness in relationship. Previously, the romance filled up the space in our lives and kept us company. We felt full because our fantasy filled in all our needs, or so we imagined.

But when we begin to really have a relationship with someone, there are gaps, there are needs not met. This is the ground for the relationship. When there is that quality of separateness and sanity, a very magical chemistry can emerge between people. It is unpredictable and unknown, and it does not follow the mythic guidelines for romantic love.

When we begin to see the other person, there is a new opportunity for romance in a sane sense. The lover's very otherness can attract us. It is fascinating what makes my husband furious, what makes him laugh. He really likes to garden, he really hates to shop. Continual fascination can bloom, because the other person is beyond our boundaries of expectation and conceptualization. That fascination can include moments of depression, discouragement, and resignation. It also includes moments of humor, delight, and wonder. But all of it is tangible and vivid. Even while we are intoxicated with the continual emergence of the other person, we are haunted and enveloped by our own aloneness.

And, perhaps surprisingly, there is an opportunity for boundless passion when you are not trying to fit someone into a role. This can be happy passion, because it is not trying to manipulate the lover into filling one's needs; it is passion that can include sexuality without fear of intimacy. It is also the vertigo of high-altitude passion, because one's own aloneness remains and the situation is so inescapable.

When you look at relationship beyond disappointment, you can begin to relate to the vivid phenomenal world. Your mate can become a symbol or representative of the entire cosmos. When he or she says "no" and is furious with you, you are actually getting a message from your world. When strain or difficulty occurs, it is very tangible and must be worked with. Everything that takes place in your relationship can become a message from the world at large.

It seems so much safer to stay romantically involved. But if we do, we will never get outside our own minds. We'll always be wrapped up in our conceptualization of romantic love. Disappointment is a loss of innocence. And that loss can actually wake us up, if we are willing to stick with the situation. There is a choicelessness that grows when you can appreciate the other person for who they are and give up trying to make them fit the image of your fantasy.

When we let go of our manipulation, relationships are fundamentally groundless. We have no control over them. In a healthy relationship, you try to support the goodness and the dignity in the other person. You don't allow them to cover up the situation again and again; you give up your feeling of betrayal if they do the same with you. You are willing to be a gentle reminder of the way things are, and allow them to be one too. But there are no assurances about your respective roles.

Should we cut romantic love out of our lives? Of course not. The intelligent way of working with romantic love is to experience it fully, beginning with the romantic passion, and then experience the disappointment and go on from there. We should understand fully what we are doing, being aware of our tendencies toward delusion when we are "in love."

There is tremendous energy in our passion. Romantic love is the beginning of understanding the nature of relationship. With it, we develop the courage to jump in, and once we are in the ocean, we learn to swim. Without romantic love, we might never have jumped in.

Falling in Love

NORMAN FISCHER

In the beloved, we find something unlimited—a feeling of connection and destiny that dissolves our selfishness and isolation. According to Zen teacher Norman Fischer, in a world of impermanence, love can be the one constant.

THERE IS NOTHING more miraculous to me than the experience of looking at a baby, especially if the baby is your own, but any baby will do. The perfect fingers and toes with their tiny, precise nails; the intense face with its soulful expression, devoid of defensiveness or posturing; the round, soft body always alive with motion or utterly in repose: a picture of pristine humanness that delights the eye and heart.

Parents can spend hours gazing at their babies with endless fascination. How could such a creature exist, and where could it have come from? How is it that it seems to look exactly like so many different relatives at once? How can its personality be already so clear and at the same time so unformed? The very nature of our lives seems to be called into question by this small person, whose fierce impulse simply to exist makes everything pale by comparison.

To really look at a baby in this way is to feel with immediacy a powerful, selfless, healing love that astonishes you with its purity and warmth. Overcome by it, you easily lose yourself in wonder. This is because the baby evokes an experience of pure human possibility.

The same feeling comes over us when we fall in love. The beloved doesn't appear as simply another person: she is rather the occasion, the location, of something unlimited, a feeling of connection and destiny that dissolves our habitual selfishness and isolation. We are overcome with a warm and enthusiastic feeling that cannot be denied and that will distract us day and night. We exist in a special zone of delight as a result of this encounter with the unexpected force of love. All songs, soap operas, and most stories feed on whatever memory or longing we have for this feeling.

But we don't decide to fall in love with our mate or our child; it is something that happens to us willy-nilly, a force of nature whose source is wholly unknown. The Buddhist sutras call it "unproduced," which is to say, unconditioned, unlimited. We can't even say it exists in the ordinary sense of that word (and this is why many people doubt that it exists as anything more than a youthful delusion). It lifts us up, releases us from all that holds us to earth. Love occurs, we now know, although we don't know what it is. We only know that we have been overcome by it.

Love is generated from twin impulses. Buddhism calls them emptiness and compassion; we could also call them wonder and warmth. Emptiness points to the miraculous nature of phenomena: that things are not what they appear to be; that they are, rather than separate, connected; that they are, rather than fixed and weighted, fluid and light. When we see a baby, when we look at the face of our beloved, we know that the way we've been conditioned to perceive the world isn't right: the world is not a fearful and problematic challenge; it is, instead, a beautiful gift, and we are at its center always.

This comes to us primarily not as a thought, or even as an emotion, but as a physical experience so compelling that we are overcome with an impulse to merge with another and, through that other, with the whole world. We want to pour ourselves out of ourselves and into the beloved, as if our body were water. Love, then, is quite naturally and positively connected with the sexual. Minds don't love, nor do hearts. These are abstractions. Whole bodies love, and naturally we want to cuddle, kiss, touch, hold, and feel the literal warmth of the other penetrate our body.

It is a wonderful and a necessary thing to hold your child next to your cheek or heart, to lie down with her at bedtime, kiss good night, perhaps fall asleep together. Such a thing is wonderful for parent, wonderful for child—this big feeling of peaceful security, of belonging, and of transcendent warmth. A person can spend a lifetime longing to return to this feeling. In the same way, it is utterly relieving and necessary to fall into the sexual embrace with the beloved, to enter each other with warmth and delight and, finally, peaceful release. It takes enormous trust to give yourself in this way, with nothing held back. It's a form of liberation. There's no sense of control, reserve, or separateness. There's no one there who could stand aloof.

I am sure that what I am saying here is so, but I also know that it is not what most of us experience most of the time. Sexuality may be the natural expression of a pure and selfless love, but it is also, in the deep economy of human emotion, chameleon-like; according to inner conditions, it takes on many colors. Clearly, the body only seldom operates in the pure service of selflessness. More often, the liberative signals that are always potentially present, because we can at any moment fall in love with the whole world, get distorted by confusion of ego. We become conditioned to see sexuality as a replacement for so much else in our lives that we need but are unable to come into contact with. So sexuality becomes, among other things, a way to express a need for power, a way to avoid loneliness, frustration, or fear. Probably nothing produces more self-deception, and when sexuality is deeply self-deceptive, it becomes dark and is the source of enormous suffering.

The Buddha respected sexuality very deeply, I think, and saw its potential for disaster. He felt that though the spiritual path naturally and beautifully contains an erotic element, the chances for perversion of the erotic are very great. Because of this, he taught the practice of celibacy as the path toward love. In fact, I would say that if celibacy is not a loving and warm practice, it is not a true celibacy; it is only a justification for a coldness or distance that one naturally prefers, perhaps out of a fear of others. But a true celibate practitioner is free, because he or she is not attached to any one or several particular persons, to develop a universal love and warmth that includes self and everyone, all held in the basket of the Way.

For those of us who do not or cannot choose a path of celibacy, the challenge is to include our beloved or our family as a part of our practice, as exactly an avenue for the development of wide and broad love for the whole world. The fact is that there is no way that love can ever be narrow or exclusive. There is a tendency to see love in a limited way, as if, if we love or are loyal to one person or group, we cannot love or be loyal to another.

But this is a perversion of love's real nature. Love's salient characteristic is that it is unlimited. It starts locally but always seeks to find, through the local, the universal. If that natural process is subverted, love becomes perverted: it must either grow or go sour. It can't be reduced or hemmed in.

It is very common, of course, for the initial pure impulse toward love to become reduced, to find ourselves domesticating the beloved, as if they were known and predictable, subject to our needs, possessable. Once this happens, there is jealousy, selfishness, disappointment, the desire to control, and the fear of change. What was once love becomes a mutual conspiracy of smallness, and nothing is more common among long-lasting and seemingly successful relationships than this embattled holding on to the past in a way that is usually quite unhappy. It is debatable whether this is preferable to the endless seeking for the perfect mate that goes on among those who see divorce or breakup as the better remedy for inner restlessness.

These are, unfortunately, the usual paths that intimate relationships take, and it is astonishing to me that the power of love and longing for love are such that people keep trying in the face of such painfully poor odds.

The alternative is to see that it is absolutely necessary to practice renunciation within the context of loving relationships. This means that we are willing to give the beloved up, to recognize that we can never really know her, or, in any absolute sense, depend on her, any more than we can depend on our own body or on the weather. She is a mystery and, as such, unpossessable, so giving her up is not a matter of sacrifice.

If we had our eyes open from the start, we would have seen that the real vision of love was showing us this all along. All things are impermanent, created fresh each moment and then gone. This being so, the miracle of love between two people or within a family is something precious and brief. In fact, any human relationship is brief. We are together for a while, and then inevitably we part. To love someone truly is to recognize this every day, to see the preciousness of the beloved and of the time we have together, to renounce any clinging need for or dependency on the other, and to make the effort to open our hands, so that instead of holding on, we are nurturing and supporting.

People often wonder how it is possible, in the face of impermanence, to make a commitment to a relationship. It certainly seems logical that we either deny impermanence and assert our undying vow or accept it and move on as soon as things change. But it is exactly impermanence that inspires commitment. Exactly because things always change and we cannot prevent that, we give rise to a vow to remain faithful to love, because love is the only thing that is in harmony with change. Love is change; it is the movement and color of the world. Love is a feeling of constancy, openness, and appreciation for the wonder of the world, a feeling that we can be true to, no matter what circumstances may bring.

Although this may sound impossibly idealistic, I believe it is quite practical. To respect the beloved, to give and ask for nothing in return, in faith that what we ourselves need will be provided without our insisting on it too much, may seem like the work of a saint, but I do not think there is any other way. In order to do it, we will have to condition our ego, soften its edges, so that it becomes pliable and fearless enough to be open to what comes and to be permissive, in the best sense of that word, for another.

PART TWO

Preparing the Ground

Making Friends with Ourselves

MOH HARDIN

A longtime student and teacher of mindfulness meditation, Moh Hardin explains that building a lasting, satisfying relationship begins by learning to extend warmth and caring toward yourself.

IF WE WANT TO CULTIVATE LOVE and deepen our relationships, it is important that we begin with ourselves. These days, people are pretty hard on themselves. I speak with many people who, from the outside, appear to have everything, but when they really talk about themselves, they tell me that they feel something is missing. Many of us feel that there is something lacking in ourselves and in our lives, that something is flawed.

In the Buddhist tradition in which I study and teach, we are taught that the ground of love, the foundation of love, is unconditional friendship toward oneself. What do we mean by "unconditional"? When we have a friend, it is usually because we like the way that person is. We get along with them. Then, maybe, that person does something we don't like, and we reject them—they are no longer our friend. We avoid them; we never want to see them again. That kind of friendship is based on certain conditions, our friend being a certain way, and when these conditions are not met, we reject that friendship.

If friendship with ourselves is based on conditions such as living up to a certain image of ourselves, and then we do or think something we don't like, something we're not proud of, we might want to reject that part of ourselves, avoid it, never see "that person" again. But the thing is, we are stuck with ourselves. We can try to run away, but wherever we go, we'll be there. Every morning when we look in the mirror, we'll be there. So if we really want to make friends with ourselves, that friendship has to be unconditional.

What is unconditional friendship? It means that you can be friends with yourself, even when you don't like yourself. But that's outrageous, you say. It's a contradiction. How can you be friends with yourself when you don't like yourself?

Actually, that's the only place you can start. If you are going to wait until you live up to the image of who you think you should be, get rid of all the dark corners, be perfect, and then you can make friends with yourself, it will never happen. So we are talking about making friends with yourself as you are, not as you would like to be.

Someone might raise an objection: If I make friends with myself as I am, accept myself as I am, there will be no reason to change, to get better, to improve myself. I can just continue doing all the bad things I do.

In response, I would ask, is that really friendship? If you have a friend who is doing something that causes harm to himself or herself, or is hurting others, wouldn't you try to help that person stop doing that, help that person change? Why? For the very fact that you are their friend! Likewise, if you can make friends with yourself as you are, of course you would still like to see yourself be the best you can be.

Perhaps you are in a bad situation or an unhealthy relationship. Making friends with yourself does not mean that you should not take steps to change the situation—either to improve it or leave it. When we talk about unconditional friendship, we are not talking about not changing, but we are talking about the starting point, the basic motivation for making a change. If you are making a change because you are your own best friend, then you will accomplish something meaningful. If you are trying to change yourself because you don't like yourself, you are picking up the wrong end of the stick—and you will just keep beating yourself up with it.

Developing a Different View

Whether we are aware of it or not, we all have a view, an understanding of who we are, why we're here, and how the world works. We might believe that we have been created by God or that we just randomly occurred. We might believe that we are a result of all our previous actions and intentions (what Buddhists call karma). There are many different ways we can see ourselves, and this is what is meant by the word *view* here. Making friends with ourselves very much has to do with how we see ourselves and the world.

For example, and to provide some reference points, I would like to briefly describe three views of reality, any and all of which might have influenced how we see ourselves.

The first is the widely held view of original sin. *Webster's Collegiate Dictionary* defines *original sin* as "a radical sin often held in Christian theology to be inherited by each person as a consequence of the original sinful choice made by Adam." According to this view, there is a basic badness in us already that needs to be kept under control, suppressed. Guilt generally plays an important role in this view. How we handle this conflict between good and evil in this, our one lifetime on earth, will determine whether we spend eternity in heaven or hell.

The second widely held view is that of science and materialism. According to this view, we are simply the result of a random coming together of an egg and sperm that both carry DNA. The purpose of life is to enjoy it while it lasts, to amass material possessions, and to experience as much pleasure and security as possible. When we die, we simply cease to exist.

A third view is that of Buddhism. Our basic nature is awake and has been forever. This is called buddha nature, and all beings possess this awake quality. My teacher, Chögyam Trungpa, coined the term *basic goodness* to express in English this fundamental nature of our being. *Basic* means that this awakened nature that lies at our core does not arise based on conditions such as whether we are poor or rich, healthy or sick. It is more basic than that, or unconditioned. Original. And this basic nature never changes. Anything that relies on conditions is always changing. Take the weather, for example. The interactions of many different conditions—highs, lows, temperature, winds, and so on—give us days of good weather and bad weather, and it is always changing. If one condition, say the temperature, changes by a degree, everything changes. But whether the days are sunny or stormy, up above the clouds, the sky itself doesn't change. It remains the sky. The sky does not arise based on causes and conditions, so it is unconditional. It just is and does not change.

Like the sky, our basic nature never changes. And this never-changing nature is good. In the Buddhist view, the ultimate nature of reality is "all-good," a goodness that goes beyond our everyday concepts of good versus bad.

Basic goodness is the natural, clear, and uncluttered state of our being that is always at our core. It is natural in that it does not have to be created or maintained in any way. It is already here. It is clear because it sees perfectly, without any distortions, whatever is happening at this very moment, like a flawless digital video camera. It is uncluttered because it is empty of all the schemes and paranoia of our ego's storylines. This natural, clear, and uncluttered state of being is always present, always there at the base.

This basic goodness naturally possesses qualities such as love, compassion, intelligence, gentleness, and wisdom. It is inseparable from these qualities, like the sun is inseparable from its light and warmth. In the Buddhist view, confusion and suffering arise from separating ourselves from the basic goodness of all life and becoming attached to protecting that sense of a separate self. Buddhists call this process "ego." Another way we could describe ego is that we tend to build a kind of fortress around ourselves that we think will protect us from life's upsets and sorrows, but in fact, it inhibits our ability to love. Feeling the need to protect our self can give rise to negative emotions such as anger and jealousy, but these emotions are not our true nature. Although they can grip us strongly, in reality, negative emotions are not who we are. They are like passing clouds that arise from causes and conditions. These clouds can cover the sun, but because they are fundamentally separate from the sun, they never affect the sun. As soon as there is a gap in the clouds, the sun shines through.

How do we bring out this basic goodness in our lives? We begin by cultivating an attitude of unconditional friendship with ourselves. We are worthy people. With that attitude, we can make an internal gesture of friendship to our self in any moment.

A Gesture of Friendship

It is like this. If we have had a bad day and are feeling flustered, angry, and upset, and if in that state of mind, a mother asked us to hold her newborn baby, we would naturally hold it gently. Why? Because that newborn life is so obviously precious and fragile. Likewise, no matter how difficult our problems may seem, no matter the obstacles we face, our lives are actually precious and fragile, just like that baby. Sometimes it's hard to believe, but we started out as one ourselves!

Our lives are precious because we experience love and compassion. Our lives are fragile because we are all going to die, and the time of our death is unknown.

We have grown up, but these fundamental qualities of our lives—precious and fragile—have not changed. So we can still hold ourselves with gentleness. We can be our own best friend. Like picking up a newborn baby, we can make a gesture of friendship to ourselves.

A gesture of friendship to yourself, like any gesture, is not just going to happen on its own—you have to do it. This is an internal gesture; you can't see it, but you can feel it. It takes place in the present moment.

To bring these words into experience, it might be helpful to compare this internal gesture of friendship to an external, physical gesture other than holding a newborn baby—let's say, the way you would gesture for someone to enter a doorway before you. A simple gesture of the hand and arm conveys, "You are there. Please go first. I will follow." When we do this, we assume a certain posture, perhaps we turn our head and body toward the other person with a slight bow; then there is the gesture itself, the movement of the hand and arms; and then the gesture ends with assuming a different posture, one of following the other through the doorway.

The initial posture acknowledges the person you are gesturing to and gets their attention: "You are there." Likewise, in making an internal gesture of friendship, we begin by acknowledging *our* presence and getting *our* attention. This means that the first step is to feel our self, however we might feel. Be aware of yourself from the top of your head down though your body to your feet and your contact with the earth. Very quickly, like the brush of a feather, scan your body and be aware of how you feel—good, bad, emotional, depressed, angry, in love, anxious, peaceful—whatever it might be. Allowing our self to feel our self is, in itself, gentleness. Nothing extra called "gentleness" need be added. That is the initial posture.

There might be a misconception that gentleness is an expression of weakness, but this gentle posture is one of strength. Why? Because you do not have to hide from yourself. From this posture, you can be kind to yourself.

In the external gesture of inviting someone to go first, from the initial posture of acknowledging the other person, you move your hand and arm in a sweeping gesture of opening, inviting the other person to go through the doorway before you: "You are there. Please go first." Likewise, from the posture of gentleness and strength, you can make a sympathetic, internal gesture of unconditional friendship to yourself as you are in this very moment. When a person is kind, they are interested in another's welfare. In this case, take an interest in your own welfare, your own well-being. Kindness feels soft, not hard. Kindness includes acceptance, intelligence, and love. Being kind to yourself is a gesture of unconditional friendship.

When someone is kind to us, it brings an experience of warmth. It might be a very simple thing. To take our example from the other point of view, if someone pushes ahead of us to go through the door first, it makes us feel bad. But if they gesture us to go first, even that little acknowledgment can produce a feeling of warmth and friendship, even if we don't know that person. Perhaps we stand up a little straighter. Even if just for an instant, we feel good. Likewise, the result of making a gesture of kindness to our self is a feeling of warmth.

The external gesture of "please go first" ends in a posture of openness: "I will follow." The internal gesture of kindness also ends in a posture of openness, openness to ourselves and some experience of warmth toward ourselves and our world.

This experience of warmth might be a physical sensation that is quite definite, or sometimes for some of us, it might be very subtle. Sometimes you might not "feel" anything. If the habit of being hard on ourselves is deeply engrained, it may take some time to uncover the natural warmth of an open heart. This path of opening occurs in the present moment and begins with a gesture of friendship to ourselves, but one gesture cannot undo years and years of training and practice in being hard on ourselves. So we need to repeat the gesture again and again, intentionally cultivating the habit of kindness to ourselves rather than hardness.

Each time we make a gesture of friendship to ourselves, we infuse our being with warmth, wholeness, and love. It's important to understand that this is a path, not a one-shot deal. Maybe at first you don't feel any warmth, then another time you have a subtle, fleeting glimpse of it. Maybe sometimes you can really feel a sense of warmth and openness toward yourself. All these experiences are all part of your journey.

EXERCISE: MAKING A GESTURE OF FRIENDSHIP TO YOURSELF

Here's a summary of the three stages of making a gesture of friendship toward yourself.

1. With gentleness, begin by acknowledging and feeling yourself as you are in this very moment.

2. Continue with a gesture of kindness and friendship to whatever that is.

3. Experience this sense of friendship and warmth within yourself.

Or, more simply, the three steps are

1. Gentleness

2. Kindness

3. Warmth

When we become familiar with this gesture of friendship, it is a simple gesture we can make to ourselves many times a day.

Having looked at it closely in this way, it is important to emphasize that a gesture, although it may have various ingredients, happens all at once. When we gesture for someone to go first, we don't have to think, "First I take a posture of acknowledging them, then I move my hand and arm, and I end up in a posture of openness." It is one gesture. We just do it. And it takes only a second. Having made the gesture, we don't try to hold on to any result.

Likewise, once we become familiar with a gesture of friendship to ourselves, we don't have to think, "Gentleness, kindness, warmth." One gesture contains all of these ingredients. We just do it. And it takes only a second. We don't try to hold on to any result but simply continue what we are doing.

We can make this gesture many times in a day, especially when we find we are being hard on ourselves. Just do it and let go. Later, do it again—and again and again.

Spending Time with Yourself

If you are interested in someone and want to make friends with him or her, the first thing you want to do is spend time with that person. Likewise, if you want to make friends with yourself, the most powerful way for that to occur is, quite simply, to spend time with yourself. The age-old practice of sitting meditation is a great way of spending "quality time" with yourself.

Simply sit down with yourself in a comfortable, upright, and attentive posture, just as if you were on a date with someone you wanted very much to get to know. Sit down with that kind of attention, and spend time with yourself.

Of course we are with ourselves all the time in some way, but usually we are busy doing something or we are distracted or we want to be entertained. We know what we like and don't like, but do we really know ourselves? Are we friends with ourselves?

Take just a few minutes each day to be with yourself in a simple way, without busyness, distractions, or entertainment. Just sit down and be. How does this work? First, it's important to take what is called a "good seat." This means that we are purposeful and deliberate about where and how we sit. Sit in a quiet place where you won't be distracted. You can sit on a meditation cushion (a *zafu, gomden,* or other cushion) or in a chair. Either way, assume an erect, comfortable posture. During sitting practice, our upright posture will provide a reminder of what we're doing, of our noble commitment to simply be for a while.

Having taken your seat, be aware of the environment and space around you, the room you are sitting in.

Then direct your focus to your breathing. The breath is a manifestation of being alive, and it always takes place in the present moment. When we place our attention on the breath, we synchronize our mind with the present moment. We become aware of being alive.

Resting on the breath, on the present moment, is like sitting on an island in the midst of a river with strong currents. All along, we have been swept along with the currents, not having any idea how fast we were going, but now, suddenly, we have a reference point, like sitting on an island. We can watch the currents of thoughts and emotions flow past. Generally, there are quite a lot of them. We will be swept away by them again and again, but by coming back to the breath, the island of the present moment, we will begin to gain a bigger and clearer perspective on the currents of our life.

Providing time in our lives for simply sitting, we become more aware, not less. So sometimes that open time of meditation may allow a memory to come up in our awareness that we have been holding under the surface and would rather forget. This is also just the process of making friends with someone else. Perhaps at first, our new friend just tells us the good stuff, but as we spend more time with him or her and become closer friends, if we really get to know this person, there is always what we would call the negative, the painful, that eventually emerges. The same will be true of ourselves—we will see the good and the bad. The mind of friendship can encompass all of it.

I would like to say that taking some time each day with yourself is the kindest thing you could ever do for yourself. It will also bring benefit to your family, friends, and everyone you love.

EXERCISE: TEN-MINUTE SITTING MEDITATION

In a quiet, undistracted place:

1. Take your seat.

2. Be aware of the room and space around you.

3. Make a gesture of friendship to yourself.

4. Place your awareness on the flow of your breathing. Identifying with the present moment in this way, watch the currents of thoughts, emotions, and worries rush by.

Many times you will be swept away in the currents, but the breath is always there, so you can come back to it again and again. A resting place.

After ten minutes, look around the room and slowly get up.

Try to do this daily. Ten minutes is suggested, but it can be shorter or longer, depending on your schedule.

THE JOURNEY OF FRIENDSHIP

Making friends with ourselves is an ongoing journey. It is not a onetime thing or a one-week project or even a five-year project. It provides the continuity of the human journey itself. It is like the ground that we walk on.

We have discussed the notion of unconditional friendship with ourselves, that we are worthy of receiving such friendship because our nature from beginningless time has been good, and two tools we have been given to help us on this journey—(1) making a gesture of friendship to ourselves in any given moment, and (2) synchronizing our body and mind in the present moment in sitting meditation. The principles we learn from using these tools, being simply present and being kind to ourselves, will be helpful on whatever journey we may embark on. It may be a business venture, a love affair, a religious quest, a spiritual path, or getting up in the morning to start a new day. I can personally say that whenever I have remembered these two principles of being present and kind, they have always been relevant and helpful.

In the Buddhist tradition, the path of love and awakening is understood to be a path of transformation. Transformation is not based on trying to change ourselves because we are bad and want to be good. It is not based on trying to change ourselves because we don't have something and need to get it. Nor is it based on getting rid of something we shouldn't have. Transformation is different than that. Transformation is a natural process that arises from basic goodness: it is a process of uncovering what we most truly are.

We need to be willing to change, or else transformation cannot occur, but that change is not based on trying to become something other than what we are right now, this very moment. The path of transformation is based on being our own best friend. Making a gesture of friendship to ourselves in any moment grounds this journey in reality and provides a stepping stone.

Recognizing Our Basic Goodness

Tara Brach

We can't punish ourselves into being better, more lovable people. But by holding ourselves with the compassion of forgiveness, we can discover that goodness is our intrinsic nature. This, says psychologist and mindfulness meditation teacher Tara Brach, is the gateway to seeing the goodness of others.

AMY ARRIVED AT HER THERAPY SESSION flushed and agitated. During the two months I'd been seeing her, she had been quiet, almost repressed. The main issue we'd worked on together was her lack of self-worth. In this session, Amy launched into telling me how she discovered that her husband had been having an affair. Over the past half year, he'd been spending an increasing number of weekends away on "work-related projects." Suspicious, Amy had decided one day the previous week to look through the e-mail he received on his company account. Numerous messages from one woman, a colleague at work, had a tone of intimacy that left her shaking with rage. When Amy confronted Don that evening, he went pale and then, looking defeated and sad, nodded and said, "You're right. It's true." He wanted to keep talking, to explain, but she couldn't listen. She told him it was all over and that she'd never be able to forgive him.

After admitting his infidelity that first evening, Don ended the affair. He pleaded with Amy to forgive him, to give their marriage a chance. Too angry to give him any assurances, Amy at first maintained a stony silence. Later she told him that if it weren't for their daughter, Celia, she would already have ended the marriage.

Ever since that night, she said, her mind had been flooded with thoughts about how he had misled her, telling her he needed to attend a conference or stay late at work or go to a team planning meeting. Her anger at being betrayed burned in her chest like an immense red fire. He was a sleazy liar. A heartless fiend. Everything he said was part of a web of deception. The whole marriage was a sham.

When we have been betrayed, one of our first reactions is to lash out in blame. We create a story of good and bad and aim our anger at the one who has caused us pain. With deep resentment, we build a case against them, often with enough evidence to prove we should eliminate them from our life altogether. The word *resentment* means "to feel again." Each time we repeat to ourselves a story of how we've been wronged, we feel again in our body and mind the anger at being violated. But often enough, our resentment of others reflects our resentment of ourselves. When someone rejects us, he or she might be reinforcing a view we already hold—that we're not good enough, not kind enough, not lovable enough.

While at first Amy focused her resentment and anger on Don, she soon turned them against herself. Don's affair had confirmed her worst fear: she deserved to be thrown aside. Every way in which she felt inadequate was reinforced by his rejection. She might appear warm and caring to the world, but inside she felt fake, wooden, grotesque. Don was the one who knew her best, and he had rejected her. Now, lost in the trance of unworthiness, Amy was convinced she was unlovable.

Especially when things seem to be falling apart—we lose a job, suffer a serious injury, become estranged from a loved one—our lives can become painfully bound by the experience that something is wrong with us. We buy into the belief that we are fundamentally flawed, bad, and undeserving of love. Like Amy, we forget our goodness and feel cut off from our heart. The Buddha taught, however, that no matter how lost in delusion we might be, our essence, our buddha nature, is pure and undefiled. Tibetan meditation master Chögyam Trungpa writes, "Every human being has a basic nature of goodness." Basic goodness is the radiance of our buddha nature—it is our intrinsic wakefulness and love.

This doesn't mean we can do no wrong. But in sharp contrast to our cultural conditioning as heirs of Adam and Eve, the Buddhist perspective holds that there is no such thing as a sinful or evil person. When we harm ourselves or others, it is not because we are *bad* but because we are *ignorant*. To be ignorant is to ignore the truth that we are connected to all of life and that grasping and hatred create more separation and suffering. To be ignorant is to ignore the purity of awareness and capacity for love that expresses our basic goodness.

To recognize this basic goodness in everyone takes courage. Trungpa calls this the task of the spiritual warrior and says that the essence of human bravery is "refusing to give up on anyone or anything." This can be especially hard when we're trying to see the goodness in a murderer, the CEO of a corporation that pollutes the planet, a child molester. Basic goodness can be buried under an ugly tangle of fear, greed, and hostility, and seeing it doesn't mean overlooking harmful behavior in ourselves or others. To radically accept life depends upon clearly seeing the full truth of it. Novelist and mystic Romain Rolland says, "There is only one heroism in the world: to see the world as it is, and to love it." Seeing the world as it is means seeing not only the vulnerability and suffering of each person, but also the basic goodness of each person. When we embrace ourselves and others with acceptance, we are seeing past the roles, stories, and behaviors that obscure our true nature.

Seeing the goodness in others begins with seeing the goodness in ourselves. Even when we feel ashamed or depressed, resentful or insecure, we don't give up on ourselves. In traditional Buddhist teachings, there are formal meditations designed to reconnect us with the goodness and loving awareness that is our true nature. These often begin with forgiveness, for it releases the armor of resentment and blame that surrounds our heart and prevents us from feeling the goodness in ourselves and others. The practices of loving-kindness awaken the love that is the flower of our goodness.

The acceptance at the center of these practices depends upon a leap of faith. Our body may be filled with painful emotions, but instead of running away, we entrust ourselves to the healing power of compassionate presence. We may have protected ourselves by closing our heart, but instead, for the sake of love, we refuse to push anyone, including ourselves, out of our heart. When we are willing to leap, our faith is not disappointed, for when we peel off the layers of delusion, we find the goodness and love that are always there.

At our next session, Amy poured out a litany of her personal failings. She was an inadequate mother. She was a bad wife. Everywhere—at home, at work—she was a fumbling, failing person. She was acutely aware of how distant she and her fourteen-year-old daughter, Celia, had become from each other. They seldom really talked, and Amy knew little about what Celia thought or felt. It shouldn't have been such a surprise that Don would turn to another woman. Who would want to be faithful to someone as bitchy and selfish as she was? She was always criticizing how messy he was, the way he planned their vacations, the way he drove the car. A particular episode stood out in her mind. One night during the past year they had been lying in bed together, and Don had started telling her about an argument he'd had with his boss. Amy had interrupted angrily: "Okay, just say it. Did you go and ruin your chances for a promotion? Did you screw up?" Don got out of bed and stood for a moment in the dark. "No, Amy," he said simply and left the room. He didn't come back to bed that night or the next. After telling me this, Amy sat back and looked down at the floor. In a weary voice, she said, "I don't know who I am more mad at—Don or myself."

Whether our anger and resentment are directed at another or at ourselves, the result is the same—it removes us from the deeper pain of our hurt and shame. As long as we avoid these feelings, we remain trapped in our armor, locked away from love for ourselves and others.

The way out begins with acceptance of our pain. When we release our stories of blame and let ourselves directly experience the feelings of shame and fear in our body, we begin regarding ourselves with compassion. Rather than living in reaction to past events, rather than identifying ourselves as an angry person, a betrayed person, a bad person, we free ourselves to meet the present moment with wisdom and kindness. This is the essence of forgiveness. Whether we are angry with ourselves or others, *we forgive by letting go of blame and opening to the pain we have tried to push away.*

But when we have deeply turned against ourselves, forgiveness can seem impossible. I asked Amy, "Do you think you could forgive yourself for being that critical person, for making those mistakes?" She responded without hesitation, "No! Forgiving myself would just let me off the hook. How would that make me a better mother or a better wife?" I gently continued, "Is there anything else that stops you from forgiving yourself, Amy?"

With some bitterness, she replied, "Why should I forgive myself? It wouldn't help those I've already hurt. I've already ruined my family. It's too late." But I knew that a part of Amy desperately wanted to remove the noose of self-hatred around her neck. I asked, "What would happen if, just for a short time, you put aside your story of being a bad person?" She said she didn't know, but she was willing to try it.

As I guided her to placing her attention on the feelings in her body, Amy said she felt as if she were dropping into a deep hole of shame, a swamp of badness. Within moments, a memory from years ago sprang into her mind. Amy saw herself in her office at home, irritated by Celia's persistent whining. She literally dragged her daughter by one arm into their den and, turning on the TV, forbade her to leave the room. She left her locked in for two hours, ignoring her periodic cries to be let out. After telling me this, she asked, "Tara, how am I supposed to forgive myself for treating my child like that? I feel so ashamed of myself."

I suggested to Amy that, instead of trying to forgive *herself*, she might just send a message of forgiveness to the shame. "Can you forgive the shame for existing?" I asked. Amy nodded, then whispered, "I forgive this shame. I forgive this shame." She was silent for what seemed a long time, so I asked what was happening. "Well," she began slowly, "it doesn't feel like shame anymore. Now it's more like fear." I let her know that she could be with the fear in the same way, letting it be there, feeling it, offering it forgiveness. After a few minutes, Amy said, "I know what I'm afraid of— that I'll never be close to anyone. I push everyone away. I don't want anyone to see what I'm really like." Crying, Amy covered her face. I gently reminded her to forgive this too, the fear and now this grief. If she wanted, I told her, she could simply say, "Forgiven, forgiven." Hugging her knees into her chest and rocking back and forth, Amy forgave and opened to the grief that had lain buried under her resentments. "There were so many times when I could have been loving but wasn't—with Celia, with Don, with my friends."

No matter what appears—burning rage, gnawing anxiety, cruel thoughts, or utter despondency—by offering forgiveness directly to each, we give permission to our inner life to be as it is. Rather than forgiving a "self," we forgive the experiences we are identified with. While resistance keeps us stuck by hardening our heart and contracting our body and mind, saying, "I forgive this," or "Forgiven," creates a warmth and softness that allow emotions to unfold and change.

When her grief finally subsided, Amy's body became very still, her face relaxed. She let her head rest against the back of the chair, and her breathing grew long and slow. When she looked at me, her eyes were red and swollen, yet peaceful. Still curled up in her chair, Amy told me about coming home from second grade and finding a stray dog sniffing around their garbage. It was "love at first sight," she said, and when it seemed her parents were going to take the dog to a shelter, Amy cried and cried. As it turned out, the family adopted Rudy, and he became the first of a string of stray creatures—including several more dogs, kittens, and an injured bird—that Amy took into her care. Amy's face softened as she said, "Everyone used to say I was so kind to animals. I just loved them. They were my friends." She joked about how Don's mild but real allergies were the only line of defense against her now creating a full-blown menagerie.

Then, in a quieter voice, she said, "You know, I do care about people, about animals. I've always been like that." As she spoke these words, I could tell that she was beginning to open the door to her own healing: "Amy, you *are* a good person. I hope you can let yourself trust this." I asked her if she had any photographs of herself with her pets. If so, she might spend some time with them. She might also take a look at some of her baby pictures, just to see what she noticed.

As we ended the session, I reminded Amy that forgiving ourselves and learning to trust our goodness can take a long time. I told her that some days I need to forgive myself over and over—twenty times, thirty times. I usually don't use a formal meditation to do so; I simply recognize that I'm judging or disliking myself and bring compassion to the pain I'm feeling. I consciously hold the intention to let go of blame and try to be more kind to myself.

Each night before going to sleep, I suggested, she might do a "forgiveness scan," scanning to see if she was holding anything against herself from the day. She might have made a mistake at work or said something condescending to her husband. If she realized that she was down on herself, she could feel the pain of her self-blame, the fear or anger or shame, and send the message "Forgiven, forgiven." She might also gently remind herself that she was doing the best she could.

With time, forgiving ourselves utterly transfigures our life. We all know stories of prisoners on death row who, through honestly facing the suffering they caused, were able to forgive themselves. By opening to the enormity of pain, their hearts became tender and awake. Other inmates, guards, prison chaplains, and relatives could recognize the glow of their inner freedom. These prisoners were not letting themselves off the hook. While taking full responsibility for their actions, they were also able to recognize the truth of their basic goodness.

We might worry, as Amy did, that forgiving ourselves is in some way condoning harmful behavior or giving ourselves permission to continue in hurtful ways. When we forgive ourselves, we are not saying, "I couldn't help doing what I did, so I might as well forget about it." Nor are we pushing away responsibility when we release our blaming thoughts. Feeling guilty and bad about ourselves for something we've done might temporarily restrain us from doing harm, but ultimately blaming and hating ourselves only leads to further harmful actions. We can't punish ourselves into being a good person. Only by holding ourselves with the compassion of forgiveness do we experience our goodness and respond to our circumstances with wisdom and care.

Amy barely spoke to Don for the next few weeks. He was sleeping on the living room couch, and she wasn't really sure what to do next. She told me she didn't want to end the marriage, but she just couldn't pretend everything was normal and let him get away with what he'd done. Despite Amy's pain and uncertainty, I could see in our sessions that something was shifting and opening inside her.

Amy came to our next session with a small packet of photos. She laid them out on the coffee table, and we sat side by side on the couch to look at them. One was of Amy as an infant cradled to her mother's breast, and we both smiled at the sweet, wide-eyed little person in the picture. In another, she was about two, sitting on her father's shoulders, hugging his head and laughing. Amy grinned. "You know, it makes me happy to see her happy!" In the others, taken when she was eight or nine, Amy was with her adopted friends—cuddling Rudy; lying in bed with her kitten, Sam, sleeping on her chest; carefully holding a small bird in her hands. As we looked at her with her animals, Amy told me she could remember how it felt to be a good person. "When you told me that last week, Tara, it was hard to take it in. But looking at these, I think I can feel it right now. That goodness and innocence—they're still inside me."

To even consider remembering her goodness depended on Amy's letting go of her belief that she was bad and unlovable. In our previous session, she had started the process of forgiveness, opening to her pain and holding it with compassion. She said the forgiveness scan had also helped. One night, as she remembered how distracted and inefficient she'd been with her real estate clients, she simply let herself feel the anxiety and shame in her body and forgave it for being there. Amy smiled and said, "I realized I could be uptight and still be a good person."

Every time we betray ourselves by not seeing our goodness, we break our heart. When we judge ourselves for falling short, we break our heart. Although Amy had been breaking her heart for years, she was now beginning to see her goodness and move toward healing.

Like every part of living, forgiving has its own natural process of unfolding. Often we are not ready to forgive ourselves, not able to forgive someone who has injured us. We can't will ourselves to forgive—forgiving is a product not of effort but of openness. This is why the intention to forgive is such a key element in the process. To be willing but not quite ready to forgive holds the door open a crack.

For the first six months after discovering Don's affair, Amy's hurt and rage had been so intense she couldn't imagine ever forgiving him. But as her heart opened in forgiving herself, it began to dawn on her that in time she might feel different about Don. She told me one day that she actually intended to forgive him—when she was ready.

It happened almost imperceptibly. Amy would notice how kind he was to Celia, how carefully he listened to her, and her heart would soften a little. When a friend of theirs got sick, she saw how helpful Don was, driving him to the doctor's office, getting take-out food for him each evening. And he certainly was trying hard enough to be nice to her, clearly making efforts to compliment her when she got dressed for work, making sure he told her exactly where he was going and how she could reach him when he was out of town. At dinner one night, she found herself laughing at a story Don was telling about the performance of his company's amateur volleyball team. As he went on, she remembered how much she appreciated the way he could put a comic spin on just about anything. There were still many moments when the full feeling of betrayal would sweep through her, but something was changing.

Amy wasn't sure just when it happened, but she told me that one day she found herself looking at the photographs of their wedding hanging on the hallway wall, and she realized Don wasn't really a bad person. He had made a big mistake, and maybe it had brought home something really painful to her about herself. But he wasn't evil or malicious. "There never was a moment in time when I thought, 'Okay, I forgive him,' she told me. "Just somewhere along the line, I no longer needed to push him away so hard."

It may not have been entirely clear to Amy, but I could see that, over the course of our work together, the better she felt about herself, the more open she felt toward Don. Seeing her own goodness opened her up to seeing his. As sometimes happens when one partner in a couple has an affair, over time Amy and Don did find their way back to each other and to a deeper and more honest relationship. Both had changed, but I attributed their success in large part to Amy's willingness to accept and forgive the feelings hidden beneath her sense of unworthiness.

Our intention and willingness to forgive, to let go of resentment and blame, do not mean that we excuse harmful behaviors or allow further injury. For Amy, forgiving didn't mean she approved of Don's way of expressing dissatisfaction with the marriage or in any way condoned his deceit. She insisted that they do couple's counseling, and she continued in therapy herself. Forgiving didn't mean she became a doormat or denied feeling angry at times. Nor did it mean she would sit back if her husband ever again betrayed their marriage. She could see Don's goodness and still set boundaries.

When we forgive, we stop rigidly identifying others by their undesirable behavior. Without denying anything, we open our heart and mind wide enough to see the deeper truth of who they are. We see their goodness. When we do, our hearts naturally open in love.

Choosing a Partner

David Richo

Do we truly want to be in a relationship, and if so, what do we want and need in a partner? Here, couples' therapist David Richo helps us to explore these questions and set the stage for a meaningful, adult relationship.

PERHAPS THE BEST PARTNERS come to us when we neither seek nor avoid the possibility of finding someone. We simply live in accord with our deepest needs and wishes and notice people we meet. We trust the universe and its miraculous power of synchronicity to bring us just the person who is best for us. But even more important than finding a partner is taking care of our hearts in a dating game that can be a devastating enterprise of broken promises and disappointed expectations.

Caring for ourselves while dating means not betraying our true nature in a desperate attempt to get someone to want us. We have to retain our boundaries intact if the process is not to end in self-abandonment and self-deprecation. We cannot allow anyone to take advantage of us or put us down for trying. Looking at ourselves from this perspective, we think, "I want a partner, and I am taking care of myself as the first step. I remain the sentry over my vulnerable inner self during this process, which may be quite dangerous to my self-esteem."

Yet we shouldn't be overcautious, for our sense of aliveness is directly proportional to how much we allow our longings to have their full career in our hearts. Longing is a source of motivation and thus of achievement. In a profound way, longing is our capacity to love. Our goal as healthy people is not to give up longing for a relationship but to let it be fulfilled moderately by others and follow a model of mutuality rather than neediness. After all, relationships are not meant to fulfill us completely but to provide us with ever-changing and ever-evolving resources as we move through life.

AM I CUT OUT FOR CLOSE, INTIMATE RELATIONSHIPS?

An adult commitment is a thoroughly truthful enterprise of ongoing love. It entails an unremitting willingness to keep agreements and handle obstacles by addressing, processing, and resolving conflicts. Happiness and mutual respect result. True love cannot be fooled, nor does it attempt to fool others. As mature adults, we can no longer be charmed by looks or sweet talk. All that matters is enduring mutual commitment.

Some people confuse attachment with love. We may feel attached to someone and imagine we love him; someone may be attached to us, and we imagine he loves us. But mindful love is bonding by commitment, not attachment by clinging. Being attached will immobilize us; love, on the other hand, helps us achieve a progressively effective and joyous evolution. We can also mistake dependency for connection. Insecure people may try to create a connection with us by fostering dependency through the offer of riches, humor, flattery, indebtedness, and so forth.

Not everyone is cut out for a fully committed relationship. He may not be relationship-oriented, or he may simply have no interest in doing the work a relationship requires. Some people are more comfortable with— and only psychologically calibrated for—light relationships or friendships. They are driven not by fear of intimacy but by truthful recognition that intimacy is not for them. There is no shame in not wanting a relationship. A healthy person is not one in a relationship but one in his own skin.

So many of us married out of social convention rather than out of a choice that reflected our deepest inclinations, readiness, and personality. People who have it in them only to be friends, never spouses, want the rhythms of distance *and* closeness that friendship provides. They prefer absence alternating with presence rather than continued presence. This is a legitimate option. But social pressures—once internalized—may push such a person into marriage, and the result is two unhappy people and perhaps unhappy children.

In the conventional view, living together is considered the logical goal of relating and an indicator of success. But the reality is that some people do not do well in mutual living situations, and they are better off in separate quarters even when the relationship becomes more intimate. Neighbors might have a better chance at stress-free relating than live-in partners. It is up to both partners to make the uniquely appropriate plan that fits for them. A primary goal in a relationship is to make sure it has the best chance of surviving—and that may not happen under one roof.

Marriage and family are a special vocation not meant for everyone. It is an individual, not a collective, choice. It is for those who will enjoy a commitment to lifelong working through, working on, and working within a context of family. It is equally legitimate to choose a celibate life or serial relationships without children or marriage. The issue for a healthy adult is not which choice she makes but whether it reflects her true desires and is carried out with integrity.

Qualified Candidates

Once we make our relationship choices in an adult way, a prospective partner who is unavailable, nonreciprocal, or not open to processing feelings and issues becomes, by those very facts, unappealing. Once we love ourselves, people no longer look good to us unless they are good for us.

A person is a candidate for a relationship when he is able and willing to give and receive love, to handle feelings, to make a commitment, and to keep agreements. He can forgive and let go of his ego long enough to work problems out amicably and fairly most of the time. He follows a reconciliation (not retaliation) model in his interactions. He loves you for yourself, not as the latest woman to fill the slot in his life marked "female." (Rebound relationships are especially dangerous in this regard.)

A suitable candidate will probably meet the following additional criteria:

- Lives reasonably close by

- Has no distracting ties that make true commitment impossible, such as another relationship in progress, an old relationship unfinished, or a divorce pending

- Has no active addictions

- Has no overpowering political or religious obsessions

- Wants children if you do or does not want them if you do not

- Has the sexual capacity, accessibility, and interest to satisfy you or can work on it within the relationship

- Has no disability with respect to money (such as cannot spend, earn, share, save, lend, contribute, receive)

- Is your friend and not just your sex partner; loves your company, and is compatible

- Shares interests with you

- Is on a fairly close intellectual par, so you do not have to play down your vocabulary or acumen

- Is not looking for the ideal mate (To need the ideal mate is not to want a real person—the only kind out there!)

- Does not appear to you to be ideal (You are not so infatuated that you cannot see his shadow side.)

- Has done at least half the work it takes to be healthy in life and relationships

- Satisfies the ruthless criterion that applies to all significant choices: that a relationship with him reflects and fulfills your deepest needs, values, and wishes

- Can and loves to focus on you in an engaged, lasting way (How do you know this is happening enough? You can remember the last time it happened.)

- Meets with the welcoming approval of your personal trio—your head, your heart, and your gut

Do these criteria fit your prospective—or current—partner?

WHAT ARE WE UP TO?

Unmet needs and incomplete transactions, like unfulfilled dreams and wishes, clamor for completion all our lives, hovering over most of our relationships. Thus, we have to learn how to finish our old emotional business on our own, since a partner cannot finish it for us.

What are we up to when we look for a relationship? Our apparent agenda may be the opposite of our real agenda. We have a conscious agenda when what we say we want matches what we set out to do. For instance, we say we want a relationship and we mean it, so we are willing to make a commitment. A secret agenda, on the other hand, is usually unknown to us. We have a secret agenda when we actually want the opposite of what we say we want. For instance, a woman who says she is looking for a partner becomes especially interested if a man seems unattainable. Once he becomes attainable, however, she loses interest quickly. The clue to a person's true agenda is always in how the transaction ends. In this example, the woman's real agenda—genuinely unknown to her—is not to find a partner but to conquer one and then to no longer have to want him.

Here is another example: Piers presents himself as looking for an intimate partnership. His secret agenda, however, is not to find adult intimacy, which scares him deeply. His fantasy of intimacy is to be held and cared for physically, but he is not so concerned with what his partner gets from him. Interestingly, when Piers locates someone, either she is just right and not available, or she is available but not quite right. This makes him seek further. He is disappointed but fully convinced he is looking for intimacy and not finding it. In reality, though, he is spinning his wheels.

Piers's agenda is secret even to Piers. He may be terrified of closeness. He may feel compelled to repeat an original and now habitual disappointment with women. His actions and frustrations show him where his work is, but will he ever do it? How many women will be blamed, how many relationships will go sour, before he sees? If he doesn't acknowledge his pattern, Piers will never know his own agenda, how it disables him from intimacy, how it relates to issues in his early life, or how to do the work that will free him from self-defeat.

Peter, unlike Piers, has a sincere, open agenda and no secret agenda. His fantasy is to hold and be held by someone who does not have to be perfect. When he locates a prospective partner, he asks himself, "Is she available, does she approximate what I want, and are we warming up to one another?" If she is unavailable—no matter how attractive—he doesn't waste his energy but passes her over. Peter bases his level of responsiveness on his intuitive powers of assessment. In a partnership, when beset with obstacles and conflicts, he works through them with his partner, the way an adult in a committed relationship does.

Peter and Piers illustrate the distinction between willing and wishing. To will is truly to want something, to choose both the goal and the means to the goal. This means accepting the work and the risks involved in seeing something through. To wish, on the other hand, is only to be enamored of the goal. Piers wishes for intimacy; Peter really wants it.

Both Piers and Peter may marry. Peter chooses a partner wisely; marriage truly suits him. Piers eventually marries someone with whom he can continue the game of hide-and-seek. He marries because that is what one does, making the big decision before he really knows himself. Finding a match is usually easy for people like Piers, because more people are drawn to apparent openness and availability than are drawn to authentic openness. Piers, then, will have many more candidates to choose from than Peter will. This is not because the candidates are foolish but because they are afraid. The "real thing" is unfamiliar and requires more bravery.

There is one final quality to assess in determining a potential partner's availability. A writer needs to know whether his computer is equipped with enough random access memory (RAM) to hold the volume of material he has to work with. Likewise, processing conflicts in relationships can take a great deal of emotional energy, so we need to know whether we have enough "random emotional energy" to work on the kinds of conflicts that arise in a relationship and whether our partner does also. For example, if your prospective partner has deep issues of sexual confusion and inhibition because of incest in her past, this will require serious, long-term work on both your parts if you want a happy sex life. Are you willing to do this work? Is your partner? If not, you are undertaking a project you cannot finish. Working in personal therapy or in a support group may help, but if you cannot carry the freight of your personal issues, no amount of love will create enough wind for your voyage.

The commitment to work through problems as they arise is the only sign that we truly want full intimacy. Only that commitment makes a differ-ence—not good looks, not empty words, not what we seek, not even what we find. An adult knows his limits, addresses them, and expands them wherever possible. This makes us candidates for an intensely real relationship.

Even if we did not find love and acceptance in childhood, we can find them—and give them—in a truly intimate adult relationship that allows a no-holds-barred exchange of feelings. Not all healthy relationships offer this, of course. Some partners want only a light, undemanding companionship, while others want to share their deepest feelings and experiences, both past and present. Both styles are acceptable, but it is important for us to know whether a prospective partner is seeking the same style of relationship we seek. Conflict happens in both kinds of relationships, but in the former, it is dealt with lightly and passed over, as are the gruesome dramas of one's past. In the latter, however, conflict is addressed with ruthless directness and processed with what might be unpleasant, messy feelings.

One way to know whether someone is open to working on a relationship with you is to give him this book. Notice whether he even reads it, reacts negatively or positively, and most of all, wants to discuss it and even practice its suggestions with you.

No Gain

BARRY MAGID

Most of us think that a good relationship will make our lives much better. Psychoanalyst Barry Magid explains that relationships are not a cure for life's pain, and they will never give us everything we want. But, he says, they are essential to our growth and development as human beings because they bring us face-to-face with our dependence and vulnerability.

ZEN TEACHER CHARLOTTE JOKO BECK pretty much sums up her attitude toward relationships when she says, "Relationships don't work." Rather than talk about everything we normally think that we gain from relationships, like love, companionship, security, and family life, she looks at relationships from the perspective of no gain. She focuses on all the ways relationships go awry when people enter into them with particular sorts of gaining ideas and expect relationships to function as an antidote to their problems.

Antidotes are all versions of "if only." If only she were more understanding; if only he were more interested in sex; if only she would stop drinking. That kind of thinking about relationships means always externalizing the problem, always assuming that the one thing that's going to change your life is outside yourself and in the other person. If only the other person would get his or her act together, then my life would go the way I want it to.

The wiser approach is to bring more attention to our fears and insecurities. These problems are ours to practice with, and we can't ask anyone else to do that work for us. To be in a real relationship, a loving relationship, is simply to be willing to respond and be there for the other person without always calculating what we are going to get out of it.

Many people come to me and say, "I've been in *lots* of relationships where I give and give and give." What they are missing is what relationships are actually for—what the good part is. Relationships provide the enabling conditions for our growth and development. That's particularly obvious with children. We would all agree that children need a certain kind of care and love in order to grow and develop. Nobody would say to a five-year-old, "What do you need Mommy for? Deal with your fear on your own!" The thing is that most of us are still struggling with remnants of that child's neediness and fear in the midst of a seemingly adult life. Relationships aren't just crutches that allow us to avoid those fears; they also provide conditions that enable us to develop our capacities so we can handle them in a more mature way.

It's not just a parent-child relationship or a relationship with a partner that does that. The relationship of a student with a teacher, between friends, and among community members—all of these help us to develop in ways we couldn't on our own. Some aspects of ourselves don't develop except under the right circumstances.

The Buddhist tradition asserts that we are all connected and interdependent, and so none of us can do it all on our own. Acknowledging this dependency is the first step of real emotional work within relationships. Our ambivalence about our own needs and dependency gets stirred up in all kinds of relationships. We cannot escape our feelings and needs and desires if we are going to be in relationships with others. To be in relationships is to feel our vulnerability in relation to other people who are unpredictable and in circumstances that are intrinsically uncontrollable and unreliable.

We bump up against the fact of change and impermanence as soon as we acknowledge our feelings or needs for others. Basically, we all tend to go in one of two directions as a strategy for coping with that vulnerability. We either go in the direction of control or of autonomy. If we go for control, we may be saying, "If only I can get the other person or my friends or family to treat me the way I want, then I'll be able to feel safe and secure. If only I had a guarantee that they'll give me what I need, then I wouldn't have to face uncertainty." With this strategy, we get invested in the control and manipulation of others and in trying to use people as antidotes to our own anxiety.

With the strategy (or curative fantasy) of autonomy, we go in the opposite direction and try to imagine that we don't need anyone. But that strategy inevitably entails repression or dissociation, a denial of feeling. We may imagine that through spiritual practice we will get to a place where we won't feel need, sexuality, anger, or dependency. Then, we imagine, we won't be so tied into the vicissitudes of relationships. We try to squelch our feelings in order not to be vulnerable anymore, and we rationalize that dissociation under the lofty and spiritual-sounding word *detachment,* which ends up carrying a great deal of unacknowledged emotional baggage alongside its original, simpler meaning as the acceptance of impermanence.

We have to get to know and be honest about our particular strategies for dealing with vulnerability and learn to use mindfulness to allow ourselves to experience more of that vulnerability rather than less of it. To open yourself up to need, longing, dependency, and reliance on others means opening yourself to the truth that none of us can do this on our own. We really do need each other, just as we need parents and teachers. We need all those people in our lives who make us feel so uncertain. The goal is not getting to a place where we are going to escape all that, but creating a container that allows us to be more and more human, to feel more and more.

If we let ourselves feel more and more, paradoxically, we get less controlling and less reactive. As long as we think we shouldn't feel something, as long as we are afraid of feeling vulnerable, our defenses will kick in to try to get life under control, to manipulate ourselves or other people. But instead of either controlling or sequestering our feelings, we can learn to both contain and feel them fully. That containment allows us to feel vulnerable or hurt without immediately erupting into anger; it allows us to feel neediness without clinging to the other person. We acknowledge our dependency.

We learn to keep our relationships and support systems in good repair because we admit to ourselves how much we need them. We take care of others for our own sake as well as theirs. We begin to see that all our relationships are part of a broad spectrum of interconnectedness, and we respect not only the most intimate or most longed-for of our relationships, but also all the relationships we have—from the most personal to the most public—that, together, are always defining who we are and what we need in order to become fully ourselves.

PART THREE

Being in Relationship

Marriage on a Plate

KAREN MAEZEN MILLER

Meditation teacher Karen Miller and her husband don't load the dishwasher in the same way, nor do they share many of the same opinions or habits or tastes. But the truth is, she says, they share everything.

HE STUDIED THE MODELS, rated the features, and compared the prices. He did what he does best and what I ask him to do in circumstances like this. He ran the numbers, and then he picked out the new dishwasher.

I was happy with the size (it fit), the color (it matched), and the delivery (in two days).

He was happy with something else. "The best thing is you don't have to rinse the plates," my husband said.

For the record, you have to rinse the plates. You have to scrape them to within an inch of their lives. You have to scrub them, yes, even though that constitutes a complete washing before you load the machine. And sometimes, you have to throw them. Things have to break. This is a marriage, you see. Something's got to give.

"When will you write about marriage?" I hate when people ask me that. I just don't know what to say. I've been looking at a blank page for months—all right, years—and I just don't know.

After the courtship, after the kid, after too many conflagrations to count, I just don't know how marriage is supposed to work. There are no experts in my house. More and more it seems to me that every question in life is *how* and every answer is *do*. And do, and do, and do.

You can try tidy formulas and messy compromises. You can soak the splatters overnight and hope they loosen by morning. You can stick religiously to the nonstick surfaces, and after a while, even those start to stick. You can try all the methods professionals recommend, and you still have a mess on your hands.

I've never found an easier way around it, so let me save you from expecting to find it. Forget the advertised claims. Drop the romantic illusions. Let go of your cherished ideals, the hoped-for bonds held intact by lifetime glue. For a marriage to last, you have to scour it yourself every day until not a fleck of fettuccine is left behind, and it gleams like a mirror beaming back your own reflection.

Then, put it in the dishwasher for good measure and go to bed.

I've noticed that how we load the dishwasher says everything about the difference between my husband and me. I have a system that I rather like. I put the plasticware and glasses on the top and the plates and bowls on the bottom. I use the prongs on the racks to prop things in place so that the blast from the sprayer arm reaches each piece. I don't put my stainless, restaurant-quality pots and pans in the machine, because the instructions said not to. So I wash them by hand. I wash a lot of things by hand. Like when my husband loads the dishwasher, I wash many things that come out of it by hand. I do it my way.

As you might have guessed, he doesn't fully rinse the dirty plates or cruddy bowls before he loads them, because the instructions said not to. He doesn't always use the prongs to prop things the way I think is right. He might squeeze a wineglass into the lower rack, crowd an oatmeal bowl beside it, and cantilever a stewpot over both. Then he might take the cutting board and put it crossways on the bottom, against the door, so the blast from the spray arm bounces off, pulsing out the side of the machine and soaking the kitchen floor. He does it his way.

Miraculously, it works. In the morning, I take the dirty dishes caked with dried food out of the machine and hand-wash them. The miracle does not occur in the machine. The miracle does not occur in the second wash. The miracle occurs when I don't say a word about it. It's not only what *I* do or don't do; without me knowing, he silently performs a million miracles himself.

Truly, the miracle of marriage lies in what we don't say and, deeper still, in what we don't know. Marriage takes one dishwasher and two miracle workers.

Sometimes people think I'm telling them they have to keep a marriage together at all costs. Phooey! That's something else I never say, because nothing stays put, intact, and inert forever. I only say that you have to keep waking up and washing the dishes, rinsing away your unmet expectations and stubborn resentments.

That's what helps me see my marriage for what it is: not the roaring flame we ignited, not the seamless partnership we promised, not the friendship we fantasized, and not quite what we were thinking.

It's taken me a long time to admit that my husband and I aren't each other's best friend, although friendship has never been our lot. At the onset of our midlife, long-distance courtship, after that fling as frisky strangers on vacation in Italy, I was uncompromising about our prospects. "I don't need a friend in Los Angeles," I said on the phone from Houston, a fair warning about the biological time bomb that had sent me hurtling in his direction.

The bomb went off, and shortly after our daughter was born, I spent a good bit of time assessing the collateral damage. Having a newborn is more than enough reason to break down and call it quits, but she wasn't the problem. While the baby napped, I parked myself in front of the TV to watch a hypnotic loop of *The Wedding Story*, which back then ran in repeats throughout a cable network's afternoon time slots. The episodes impaled me with doubt, because the real-life couples on the verge of their vows always had a dreamy sense of destiny, adoration, and friendship that was unlike anything I'd experienced in my own life. I worried myself heartsick. Did everyone marry a best friend but me?

My best friend was back in Texas, and if I called her and said I had a flat tire in the pouring rain in rush hour on the 405 freeway, she would climb on a plane with two umbrellas and a jack. My husband would more likely counsel me with a cool head while never leaving his engineering cubicle, "Call AAA." My marriage was not the stuff of white-horse rescues. Of course, it never rains in Southern California, and I didn't fall in love with a tow truck driver. You think my expectations were off course?

That was before I decided to give myself a break. It was before I decided that marriage—at least our marriage—wasn't about friendship at all.

Come to think of it, why would anyone want to marry a friend? I have plenty of friends, and I do not want to marry any of them. I want to go have coffee with them and talk about how my husband infuriates me. That's the place to bring it up, if at all.

No, ours is not a marriage of friends making nice. Ours is a marriage of adversaries making peace. I wonder if that's what makes this odd and uncomfortable convention so transformative: not that we marry our friends, but that we marry strangers—indeed, opposites—and then remarry one another every day. Perhaps that's what creates lifetime peace, love, and harmony: the honest effort, not the butterflies and moonbeams.

"So you mean there's no reason to get married?" says a friend whose very ceremony I performed. She is stumbling, dazed and defeated, through the scorched earth of her fourth year.

"There's no good reason at all," I say. There is no good reason to make any of the promises we make, and that's where the magic occurs. Marriage is not a choice you make like picking the glass tumblers from Crate & Barrel that promise to be dishwasher-safe. (Mine cracked anyway.)

Marriage shows us how flimsy and meaningless the reach of reason can be. It teaches us to go beyond what we think we can do—*we can do more*—and reexamine just exactly who we think is going to do it for us—*each of us, by ourselves.*

Truly, there is not much two people can share. My husband and I do not share the same opinion about many things, except certain U.S. presidents and Academy Award nominees. We don't share tastes in music or reading; we don't have the same habits; we don't favor the same religion; we don't have the same inclinations about money, except we'd both like the other to make more of it. It doesn't take very much self-awareness to see that it is impossible for two people to share the same point of view.

We seem to disagree just because we can. It's another mindless habit. In the split second after one of us speaks, there is a choice to be made: Accord or discord? Acceptance or rejection? A nod yes or a shake no? What you do or don't do in that second is the source of all second chances.

When the going gets tough, he'll say something like, "If people could see the way you really are, they wouldn't think you were so Zen." That's one thing we instantly agree on. I remind him that I don't practice meditation because I'm someone better. I practice because I'll never be anyone else.

A marriage is a lot like a silent meditation retreat anyway. In both cases, you come face-to-face with the most unlovable aspects of yourself, your messy unpleasantness, your selfishness, and the panicked impulse to duck and run. Neither experience is anything like the honeymoon you signed up for. The point is to pitch all that out and stay put. With my meditation practice, I can see that I'm still a cranky person, but I try to be a kinder cranky person. One who says less but always says, "I'm sorry."

I've been married before, and you might wonder how the second time around is better than the first. Surely the first one was wrong and the second one is right? I've stopped thinking that way. It seems to me that we have the same fights, the same frustrations, the same salty tears, the same low-grade despair, and yes, even the same loneliness. I've stopped thinking that one husband is better and one is worse, or even that my husband is different from yours. Comparisons are inherently false, distorted by our own self-centeredness, and serve no one. Besides, the way we tell it, husbands can seem uncannily alike. After two, five, ten years or more of cohabitation, we still complain about the toilet seat.

In the middle of it all, I remember that my husband doesn't claim to have a spiritual practice, so how could he see things as I do? In the middle of it all, I remember that I *do* have a spiritual practice, so why don't I try to see things as he does? I cannot find a different husband, but I can find a different me who looks at things differently, taking more responsibility and assigning less blame, appreciating the whole instead of dividing the parts.

Two people may not share many things, but the truth of it is, they can share everything.

I share my husband's humbling and terrifying love for our child.

I share his pride and satisfaction when he fixes the sprinklers, his fuming frustration when they need fixing all over again.

I share a refuge until one of us turns it into a war zone.

I share the unpredictable ride in this life of ours: the fits, the fights, the glide, and the cycles. There really are seasons, and they really are different. Take care that you do not measure the autumn by the spring.

I share the shortening horizon and the coming certainty that we will need each other's strength and gentleness over the steepest ground yet.

I share the blanket of calm, the dark secret of sleep's mysterious company.

I share his glance, his twinkle, his smile, and his touch.

I share the love that is quiet, patient, and kind, the love that bears all things and surrenders its way.

I share a pot of coffee in the morning and a sink of dishes at night.

"Do you want me to load the dishwasher?" he asks, because he so often aims to help me out.

"That's okay, I'll manage it," I say and wave him off, so caught up in my own arrogance that I've overlooked the gift. I do not say what I mean, what I still mean after all these years, the declaration that serves us without either of us knowing quite how. So I say it here before the assembled guests.

I do, honey, I really do.

Moving Target

Erik Hansen

When longtime Zen practitioner Erik Hansen pays mindful attention, he realizes his wife is constantly changing, always surprising. Beneath his conventional knowing of her, he finds a vast unknowing, and that's an openness that inspires curiosity—and leads to intimacy.

HAVE YOU EVER PRACTICED EATING MINDFULLY—let's say a salad or a baked potato? Perhaps, then, as you tried to stay in touch with each bite, each chew, each subtle flavor of potato, butter, salt, pepper, and chives, you found yourself struggling through a haze of memories, fantasies, and scenarios to really be there for the experience of eating.

Now extrapolate from this experience and think, if it's this challenging to stay in touch with a baked potato, how much harder must it be to clearly perceive the person I love? After all, my relationship to a potato is fairly straightforward, whereas my perceptions of my wife, for example, are overlaid with all kinds of control issues, power struggles, sexual bonding, primordial needs, and so on. Complicating matters is the fact that, although these forces are as real as gravity, bending my perceptions the way a black hole bends light, they are invisible. Most of the time, I don't even know they're there.

Zen practice suggests there are many degrees to being present. Just because my eyes are open doesn't mean I'm awake. It's possible to look right at someone and still not truly see them. I certainly make every effort to make contact with my wife, Shannon, whom I adore, but I've come to realize that I'm almost always peering at her through the invisible haze of my own mind.

Take Sunday. Since I'm a writer, it's important that I read widely and often, so as I pull a chair into the afternoon shade and open an Elmore Leonard novel, it's with a clear conscience. Unfortunately, my enjoyment is soon undermined by muffled sounds coming from the basement— Shannon cleaning and reorganizing. *She expects me to help her,* I realize with a twinge of annoyance. More sounds emanate. Boxes shifting. Sweeping. "It's always on her schedule," I grumble, no longer seeing the words on the page. Finally, she appears in the doorway, broom in hand, and stares at me. *Oh, all right, all right!* I put the book down and stomp to my feet, thinking, *She just doesn't value what I do.*

But as I sweep last Sunday's wood scraps from where I left them on the floor, I realize *Shannon's been stepping over these all week.* Wow. Maybe everything's not "always on her schedule." Maybe her perceptions, her trajectory through life, are just as valid as mine.

"She doesn't value what I do." At the time, it sounded almost reasonable. That's what the mind does. It makes statements and then believes them. "No one loves me." "He's a dumb brute." "You're the worst kids in the world." As my Zen teacher would say, it "conceptually ornaments" our experience, adding labels, concepts, and judgments to create a story of self and other. What we do with these thoughts is the point of our practice. Do we believe them or let them go? Do we build ever-larger conceptual edifices around our loved ones, or do we work to pull those structures down?

How clearly do you see *your* loved ones?

In the basement, Shannon decides to reposition her worktables, so we take half an hour experimenting with different configurations. As we push the tables this way and that, something interesting happens. I start to feel more fondly toward her. This low, cool space is where she spends much of her time, making art, and it's suddenly become more real to me. I'm taking care of her. I'm a good guy. I spend some time with a couple of her new pieces, appreciating them. Seeing them. You know, she's not just an inhabitant of my mind; she's here, in the world, living her separate, parallel life.

I believe we could spend our whole lives together, living like bears in a cave, grunting over salmon, sleeping in our nest, and enjoy a deep and intimate bond—but would we have made contact? I want to see past the haze, past my conceptual ornamentations, past this Shannon who's so familiar I sometimes believe she's "me" or "mine." I want to see the real her. But how can I break through?

Talking is a start. "Hey, hon. How about some iced tea?" We go outside. I bring her a tall, beaded glass of tea, again feeling that subtle pleasure of taking care. Just putting the glass in her hand helps me to feel loving. "So, Shan. Do you think you see me clearly?" I ask. She sips her tea, considering. "It's not something I worry about," she answers. Oh. "Well, take a moment," I persist. "How do you perceive me?" "Lots of different ways . . . that all have to do with me. Does that sound selfish?"

You see? I didn't know what she'd say. I never do. She's a moving target, constantly changing, frequently surprising me. The truth is, when I pay attention, I find beneath my conventional knowing of her a vast and profound *unknowing.* A big open space that inspires curiosity and leads to contact. So we sit together, my mind enjoying the not-knowing, sipping iced tea on a Sunday afternoon. For a moment, I see her without ornament.

And for the record, she in no way resembles a baked potato.

To Love and Be Loved

RABBI HAROLD KUSHNER

Rabbi Harold Kushner, the author of When Bad Things Happen to Good People, *has this advice for couples: choose happiness over righteousness. The essence of marital love, he says, is not romance, but forgiveness.*

PEOPLE NEED TO FEEL UNDERSTOOD and supported. Many members of my congregation come to me for counsel. I've learned that they are looking not for advice—often they already know the answer—but for understanding. And I give them my concern, my sense that they are worth caring about and that their problems are worth taking seriously. Receiving this message is immensely therapeutic for them.

I often see how this need simply to be loved with understanding manifests itself in married couples. The wife starts to tell the husband her problems. After a minute, he interrupts and tells her what to do about them, because he's geared up to be a problem solver. But she's very unhappy, because she doesn't want his advice. She wants fifteen minutes of his undivided attention. She wants validation that her problems are as important to him as they are to her. And if he would just hold still and listen for those fifteen minutes, she would get the message that he cares about her.

People can do this for one another, can love one another with understanding. All around me, I see many people whose lives are not as fulfilling as they might be, simply because these people are too involved with themselves. I think our society puts too much emphasis on finding someone who will love you; our culture focuses too much on being loved and not enough on being a loving person. It's much easier to be a loving person, to give away love. This ability is something you can have control over. None of us has the power to make someone else love us. But we all have the power to give away love, to love other people: if we do so, we change the kind of person we are, and we change the kind of world we live in.

This attitude is what works for me in my own marriage. The essence of marital love, I have learned, is not romance, but forgiveness—accepting a person's imperfections and understanding that each of us has his or her quirks that would drive our mates crazy but for the love between us. When I'm in a bad mood, I can only hope that my wife is prepared to write it off as just a bad mood, not the essential me.

Some years ago, I read a wonderful newspaper column. A woman sees two children in a playground get into a fight. One of them says, "I hate you. I never want to play with you again." For two or three minutes they play separately, and then they come back and start playing with each other again. The observer says to a woman sitting next to her, "How do children do that? Be so angry one moment and together the next?" And the neighbor says, "Oh, it's easy. They choose happiness over righteousness."

That is the advice I give a lot of married couples. Choose happiness over righteousness. Even if you're right, don't demand recognition of the fact. Sacrifice the victory for the sake of a happy marriage. In a happy marriage, there are no winners and losers, only two people who agree to put up with each other—exasperating as that may be.

The rewards are certainly worth it. There is a satisfaction you can find only in a marriage, as you make yourself part of a larger entity. We see this in the biblical injunction that "therefore shall a man leave his father and mother and cleave unto his wife and they shall become one." You achieve a sense of wholeness, not just when you find someone with whom to sleep and live, but when you can really join with another person and feel his or her joy, feel his or her pain. There's a sense of expansion of your own self. The emptiness in your life is filled in a way that you can't get from any other human experience.

If you work it right, possessing a sense that there is something greater than you the individual, whether it be spirituality or a child, also creates a sense of happiness and love. I think we all need some sort of force to pull us out of our narcissism and our overconcern for ourselves. Having a child can do this. I've seen how a child changes people, just knowing that this other life is dependent on them. A sense of religious commitment can do this too. It opens the heart, bringing a sense that you owe something to a cause greater than your own well-being or your own satisfactions. I think human beings are created to be this way, and when we act selfishly and narcissistically, we're acting against our essential nature. People are not meant to be selfish.

People are meant to be loving, and they are meant to be intermittently happy. I suspect that people who are happy all the time probably don't realize what's going on around them. There is so much pain in the world, only by shutting our eyes to it could we always be happy. But we do have the power to always be loving, always be caring. And from time to time, we have a moment of happiness that justifies everything that leads up to it.

This runs counter to a lot of the messages all around us: that if we just get a certain something—a better car, a better neighborhood, a better pair of sneakers—then we'll be happy. Of course, this frame of mind doesn't work. It only makes us more insecure. Advertisers need to make us feel anxious so that we'll buy whatever they're selling to make us feel better. And insecurity makes it hard for us to feel worthy of love, to believe that others will accept us if they really know us, and ultimately to be accepting of other people.

Someone once wrote, "Happiness is always a by-product. You don't make yourself happy by chasing happiness. You make yourself happy by being a good person." The happiest people I know are people who don't even think about being happy. They just think about being good neighbors, good people. And then happiness sort of sneaks in the back window while they're busy doing good.

This attitude works in relationships as well. I always worry about a relationship in which one or both parties are constantly taking the temperature of the relationship and measuring whether they're happy. I suspect that such an appraisal leads to asking questions like, "Would I be happier if I were in a relationship with somebody else?" Instead of asking themselves, "Am I happy?" I think they should ask themselves, "Is there something I can do to make this a better relationship? What else can I give to it?" If they do that enough, they'll turn around one day and realize happiness has snuck up on them.

Being loving toward others and creating a relationship in which they love us is a reciprocal process. We begin by being loving toward ourselves, seeing ourselves as capable of loving, capable of giving things away. It's a very stunted person who can't give him- or herself away emotionally because of being afraid there won't be much left if he or she does. Loving ourselves doesn't mean narcissism and self-worship. It means accepting the imperfections in ourselves and realizing that nobody expects us to be perfect. Self-love means seeing that not every mistake is a permanent stain on our self-esteem and our sense of worthiness. That's how you love yourself. I worry about people whose major goal in life is getting enough love, because I think they end up being takers rather than givers.

It helps to have some moral code in achieving these things. We act against our essential nature when we are dishonest or devious or selfish. And acting against our essential nature impinges on our ability to give and receive love and on our ability to experience happiness. For example, adultery corrodes a marriage because it introduces an element of dishonesty.

I have trouble understanding people who do things that, in the long run, are only going to hurt them. This self-damage could be in the way they eat and drink or behave with their families. Probably what is happening is that they're not confident that they'll get enough love, so they go out and steal it, just as people who feel they don't have enough money rob people. People who are worried that they're not going to get enough love try to get love by unethical means. This isn't just limited to marital infidelity. For example, a woman trying to get love by illicit means might pretend to be someone she isn't. She wears a mask when she's suppressing her own individuality, her own needs and wants. She's hoping to be loved by people who wouldn't love her if they knew what she was really like.

I don't think people who do this realize how inherently contradictory it is. How can it be real, nourishing love when it's gained dishonestly? When they are hiding their true nature? It is always a futile pursuit; it always catches up with them. And ironically, they stay hungry.

I think in the long run we love people who, by accepting us, enable us to be better than we otherwise would be. We love someone who reflects to us an image of ourselves that makes us feel good about ourselves. We love someone who frees up the creative and emotional energies that otherwise would remain dormant. We love someone, too, who helps us to be a loving person.

Some religions, like some people, have the kind of message that liberates our own ability to love. If the message of the religion is "God loves you despite your shortcomings," your heart is opened to giving and receiving love. But if the message we hear is "You have sinned, you have fallen short, you're no good. God is disappointed in you," we're going to tighten up. It turns us into emotional misers, unable to give away love. But if the message is "God knows exactly who you are and loves you anyway," we are permitted to love and to forgive—ourselves and the other imperfect people in our lives.

There are a lot of religious spokespeople who don't agree with me, but I believe that God really did make us in his own image—a model of love and forgiveness that we can emulate. This is very important. This is how I try to live my life.

I recognize that I need love in the same way that I need food and sleep and exercise. I understand that my soul would shrivel up from malnutrition if I didn't love, didn't give love and receive love. One of the things that works for me, helps me fill my heart with love, is the series of Jewish prayers that focus on being grateful for all the things around us that we might otherwise take for granted. The first words of prayer when Jews wake up in the morning are to thank God that they're still alive and awake; that their bodies work, their arms, their legs, their eyes, their minds work; that they have clothes to wear and food to eat and things to look forward to. When your heart is filled with gratitude, when you can just go out and feel how lucky you are that the world is there for you and how lucky you are that there are people out there trying to enrich your world, it's a lot easier to be loving—to yourself and to others.

Finding Forgiveness in a Ziploc

JANE HAMILTON

Novelist Jane Hamilton reflects on marriage, compassion, and making it through the security line at the airport.

ONE MORNING LAST SUMMER, I blew up at my husband in LaGuardia Airport just after we had gone through security. There was no ticking of the bomb that I knew of, no flame traveling along the fuse to the dynamite. The white-hot fury was suddenly upon me—boom, no warning. This explosion was shrill. It was loud, it was in earnest, it was heartfelt.

Our trip to the city had been fine. We had gone with a long list of things to accomplish, for pleasure and business. It was hot, but we are used to heat.

We don't travel together much, and we go forth with the knowledge that being in strange places in each other's company isn't our strong suit. I tend to dash into traffic, thinking I can surely make it to the median. My husband, who was the captain of the patrol boys in the eighth grade, has a tendency to hold out his arms at the curb: stand back!

Deep down, I think he still wants to guide everyone to safety, wearing the treasured blaze-orange harness. Also, he would prefer that I don't make lifelong friends of strangers in the museum and at the theater. Instead of trying to do everything and all at once, he favors a moderate schedule. I travel quite a bit, and he loves to stay home, and I've always hoped that, for him, part of the payoff of being married to me is the fact that through my friends who visit us, the world comes to his doorstep.

Despite our different tendencies and tempos, we had managed during that trip to be on our best behavior. When the time came to leave, we found a taxi and reached the airport with well over an hour to spare.

The line for security wasn't long. We did everything correctly: took off our shoes, held up our regulation-size Ziploc bag of toiletries and put it into the little white dish. The buzzer went off for my barrette and my underwire bra, but the authorities and I worked it out. Our carry-on emerged from the X-ray chamber and came smoothly down the line.

I suppose if there were a flame traveling the fuse to the explosive, it was ignited there, in the moment when my husband pulled the carry-on to the end of the counter.

Oh no, I thought. *Oh God.*

He picked up the Ziploc bag.

Don't do it, don't do it!

You see, he did not want to return the Ziploc to its usual place in the front compartment of the suitcase, the place I always put it. No, he wanted to find a better place, a more secure place where, in case of a tip, a toppling, the lotion and toothpaste wouldn't be squeezed out; no gels or liquids would make a mess. At the end of the metal counter, as clean and grim as a surgical table, my husband was fussing.

"Just put it back where it was," I said.

"No," he said, "it will fall out."

I have taken roughly one thousand trips with that bag without any kind of toiletry incident. Never had it occurred to me to put the goods in any other compartment. But clearly, for years, my reasoning had been faulty.

What made me blow? His need to control my baggage. The fact that I am always wrong. His laser beam on a Ziploc bag, his concern for a quart-size plastic container filled with three vials.

But most of all, it was his fingers, his fiddling hands like a raccoon's paws at a bottle cap, the way the animal obsessively turns the shiny thing over and over. That made me insane. Your Honor, I went insane. In the sanctuary that was airport security, I began to scream. "Stop it!" At the top of my lungs, I shrieked, "Just stop it now! Stop it this minute!" I didn't even quite know I was doing it, although I admit that, in the instant, the blast felt, actually, pretty good.

The poor man froze. *This is not happening.*

Oh, but it was. I was just about to bellow, "Is there a divorce lawyer in the house?" Instead, I fled down the concourse, inflamed with righteousness. He was always trying to control everything down to the smallest detail. And I could not, would not, endure it another second. This moment of outrage was not about the moment. It was about twenty-six years (twenty-six years!) of living with a strong, good, detail-oriented, iron-willed, fastidious person. This moment of outrage was the culmination of every moment.

I sat down several yards from our gate, as far away as I could get in the short concourse. I sat erect, breathing not at all normally. I wondered how I was going to get home, if I was even going to try to get home. Because our life together was over, it was done.

I did not look back up the concourse or even glance to see if he was still knitting his hands at the suitcase. As I sat doing my best to plunge further into my ire, a curious thing happened. It was as if a switch in my brain were flipped and a whole new template slid into place, the action beyond my volition.

All at once, I had a vivid sense, as best as I can judge, of what it might feel like to be my husband. For no reason that I can account for, I was suddenly looking from his eyes out into our own particular little ruined world.

Sure, I had tried to do this many times before in our years together, tried to imagine how he felt, but this was different. I was him. And I thought, how awful, how terrible this is, being him. All of my own indignation and all of my poor hurt feelings that had built up through the years were vaporized.

I knew, despite the good and joyful nuggets of our daily life, that it was a difficult—harrowing—proposition for him to live with someone who is so voluble and indiscreet and extravagantly enthusiastic, someone who is always saying, "Yes, yes, yes!" What a burden it must be, I must be, for someone who is quiet and private and focused, someone so careful in his deliberations.

I walked back to the gate to find him sitting with his magazine, looking small and hunched. What else could he do but wait?

"I'm sorry," I said simply, hoping he would see how ashamed I was, how contrite and how sad and how frightened.

Whenever I visit my doctor I read the framed poster right by the exam table called "Happiness in Love." It lists, against a background of billowy clouds and wise songbirds, recommended behaviors for maintaining domestic happiness: sensible, if impossible, bromides like "Don't go to bed angry," "Be generous," and "Forgive your spouse and forgive yourself."

At the airport, I wasn't sure we could recover from this one, wasn't sure I was forgivable. I couldn't tell him that I was now fortified with my new and improved vision, a way of being that might, if I could remember always to use it, allow for a permanent, deeper sympathy and understanding.

I couldn't explain that just as T cells in the body respond to a pathogen, so a spiritual-type corrective had somehow flooded my system. That was a change he would have to feel—oh, if only he would soon feel it. I had not willed the corrective; rather, something as irregular and beautiful and strange as grace had visited me.

Later, I was telling a friend about the whole ridiculous incident. Well, I told a bunch of friends, just as my husband mentioned it to no one. My first friend said, "But did it last, that feeling?"

Ah, that's always the rub. The recidivism rate in these matters is so high. But in my case, I'm still working to stay on the wagon. Many months have now passed, and so far I have tried to flip that switch not only when I've thought it might come in handy, but every morning, every evening, like a prayer.

I make a point to remember that the temperament of my husband, the temperament of that patrol boy, is my salvation. It is beyond the call of duty and maybe even love that he makes the effort, time and again, to keep me from running into traffic.

The second friend said, "But in order to maintain that perspective, you have to reach within yourself to such a deep place."

This is true. But like any exercise, any devotion, it's a practice. And even if it doesn't become easier, one hopes it becomes habit.

The third friend noted that you spend all this time trying to find the right man and then wondering if you should stay, and complaining about his faults, and wondering some more if you should stay, but then the day arrives when you realize you'll probably outlive him.

And it won't be just that you're alone, but that you'll be without him, that very man. In life you rue all the qualities he doesn't have, while once he's dead you'll long for each lovely trait. Both she and I, married to older men, know that we've wasted a lot of time, squandered a portion of happiness.

It is sad that twenty- and thirtysomethings, as reported in the media, are skittish about commitment. But I can imagine that long-term marriages often don't look so great to them from the outside: there she is, the crazed, middle-aged woman shrieking at her husband in the airport, she with fangs and black wings flapping, and he cowering.

But if you are lucky, there is the flip side of that meltdown, the moment not too long after, when you get on the plane and your husband asks if you have the magazine he was reading, and you say, "Yes, but I put it in the bag, and if you get it out right now, I'll have to scream and scream at you." And then you both laugh, pretty hard.

"Forgive your spouse and forgive yourself," the Happiness in Love poster counsels. Often in marriage, you have to strain to forgive. But sometimes you don't have to as much as lift a finger. Every now and again, forgiveness is just there, miraculously, for the having.

Becoming Intimate with Fear

Ezra Bayda

Until we face our fears, we will not be able to truly connect with others because we'll still be disconnected from ourselves. Zen teacher Ezra Bayda offers tools to help us touch our fear and, finally, to move beyond it.

Love is very difficult to discuss because it means so many different things to different people—from sexual love, to romantic love, to friendship love, to family love, and so on. The one thing these various kinds of love have in common is that they are all forms of personal love, where we are so often caught up in the highs and lows of emotion and attachment. But there is another kind of love, one that is not even an emotion—it is the natural state of our being. This love is what naturally comes forth when all the conditions that we add to our relationships—our agendas, our needs, our expectations—stop getting in the way.

Yet isn't it true that we rarely experience this sort of love? Isn't it much more common to experience relationships as a source of difficulty? I'm not just talking about relationships with our mates, but also with our parents, our children, our bosses, our friends, and even with strangers we interact with at random throughout the day. So why is there so much difficulty? Or, more pointedly, what is it that each of us brings to relationships that seems to cause so many problems?

The answer is: ourselves! We bring our assumptions, our hopes, and most of all, our wants. Whenever we want something from someone, which is always true when we have expectations and requirements of them, we can't really see them as people. We only see them in terms of what we want them to provide. And as long as we want something from them, our capacity for love is blocked. This might lead to difficulties around intimacy or trust, around fears of criticism or rejection, or around feeling unappreciated or controlled. Certainly money issues and sexual issues can cause us difficulties.

Given these inevitable difficulties, relationships often test us, pushing us to the edges of where we're stuck. But even though being pushed in this way is uncomfortable, it affords us the invaluable opportunity to go deeper into our life and to reconnect with the unconditional love that is our true nature. We may think that the difficulties of a relationship will prevent or distract us from our desired journey on the spiritual path; we may think that in order to know ourselves more deeply, we have to ascend the mountaintop alone. But the issues that arise in relationships can, in fact, push us in ways that we would never push ourselves on our own, in spite of the sincerity of our quest. And it's this very fact, that relationships often trigger our most painful and unhealed emotions, that makes them such a potentially useful teacher.

There are three main steps essential to working with relationships— knowing oneself, refraining and experiencing, and practicing Being Kindness. Taken together, these three steps will help us learn to live from our true nature.

KNOWING ONESELF

To see clearly what you really want from a relationship, or at least what you believe you want, think of one important relationship where you're experiencing difficulties. Now consider the following questions: What is this relationship supposed to give me? What are my specific expectations of this person?

We often want other people to be a certain way, primarily so that we'll feel a certain way, such as safe, confident, loved, pleasured, happy, appreciated, and so forth. For example, when we believe someone loves us and wants us, we not only feel loved but also worthy of love, which is often the balm we crave to cover over our basic fears of unworthiness. But if our needs and expectations are not met in that relationship, we often feel unloved, rejected, lonely, and unappreciated. Again, think of your own situation to see how this specifically applies. We need to see that almost all of our relationship difficulties come from our wanting someone or something to be different.

Often compounding or intensifying relationship difficulties is the fact that we almost always enter into relationships unaware of our expectations. I met my first wife in a spiritual community and thought at the time that I wanted nothing more than a partner on my spiritual journey. But what I also unknowingly wanted was someone to pay attention to me and appreciate me, and this lack of awareness eventually caused unending difficulties.

The point is, one of the most basic aspects of mindfulness in relationships is to become clear about our own specific expectations and agendas. We need to know, very precisely, both how we want another to be and how we want them to make us feel.

The more clearly we see our assumptions and patterns, the more our unrealistic and self-defeating views of relationship will slowly be dismantled. The surrender of our illusions—about what relationship is and particularly about what it's supposed to do for *me*—is essential. But in order to surrender, we first have to learn to see ourselves more clearly.

Again, thinking of your own particular situation, when you don't get what you want or when you get what you don't want—that is, when your expectations aren't met—what are your typical emotional reactions? Are you prone to anger, hurt, self-pity, anxiety, depression, fear? It's important to be clear about what your particular emotional reactions are; otherwise, relationships will remain a mystery, and their difficulties may seem to be unworkable.

We tend to view relationship difficulties as obstacles, as impediments to our happiness. Usually, when these difficulties arise and we get upset, we automatically believe that something is wrong. Then we jump to the belief "I have to fix this." But in doing so, we're missing a crucial point, which is seeing that these obstacles, these difficulties, can themselves be a step on the path of growth and awakening. They are not in our way so much as they *are* our way.

We often forget that difficulties present the most valuable opportunities to learn about ourselves, especially about our own barriers. In relationships, the other person is, in fact, a mirror reflecting back to us exactly what needs clarifying—our expectations, our judgments, our anger, and our fear. In this sense, rather than seeing the other person as the cause of our suffering, we begin to see that person as our teacher, indirectly pointing to what we must attend to.

But remembering to see our relationship difficulties within the context of mindfulness practice is a big, and often incredibly difficult, step. How often do we view our difficulties in this way? For example, if someone is critical toward us or betrays us, how often do we remember that they're our teacher? Yet when we don't remember this, aren't we perpetuating our own cycle of suffering and the hurting of ourselves and others?

When difficulties arise, we must first remember that this is about *us* and that our struggle is our opportunity to wake up to exactly what we need to work with. For example, as we hear thoughts such as "I can't stand it when he does that," "Nobody should be treated this way," "This just isn't right," or "Why does she always do that?" can we begin to see them as clues that mindfulness practice is necessary? This means to see them clearly as just deeply believed thoughts coming out of us, out of our conditioning. It's important to understand that our thoughts, no matter how strong, are not necessarily The Truth. And even if they sound "right" objectively, we can ask ourselves whether they in fact foster righteousness rather than relatedness.

Refraining and Experiencing

As a result of our emotional reactions in relationships, we often engage in power struggles, trying to change others to suit ourselves or withholding something they want until they give us what we want. Think of a difficult relationship. Can you see how you're often unwilling to give, primarily because you're not getting what you want, and how quickly a power struggle ensues before you're even aware of its roots?

In relationships, particularly when we have an emotional reaction, we'll almost always focus on the other person instead of looking inward. What we're really trying to do is change that person so they'll fulfill our hopes and expectations. In these power struggles, we may even view the other person as our enemy, which leads us to either erect barriers of protection or attack in order to defend ourselves. We must be honest about this.

Even when we know intellectually that our emotional upset is the result of bringing our own expectations and agendas to the situation, it is often difficult to see this clearly when we're upset. And even when we do see it, it's still difficult to work with. Why? *Because it means that we have to stop blaming others.* This point is crucial.

Whenever we find ourselves wanting to point the blaming finger at someone or something outside of ourselves, we can gradually learn to turn the finger around and look at what we ourselves are doing. This does *not* mean that we blame ourselves; it means that we stop blaming altogether.

The problem is we don't want to stop blaming. It is one of our choice detours away from reality. We often *want* to be angry, to be right. We like the juiciness and power that we feel when we're angry. But in order to work with relationship difficulties, we have to recognize the tenacity of these defensive strategies of blaming and righteousness. And here's where it gets really sticky, because once we do stop holding on to blame and defense, we are left with the one thing that we least want to experience—the quivering core of fear that we have tried all our lives to avoid. We have to realize that the reason we focus on blaming someone else is to cover over having to feel this fear-based pain. We don't want to feel the discomfort of that.

The practice emphasis is to come back again and again to our own inner process; yet it's important to note that sometimes we may encounter situations that objectively require action, sometimes even right away. But whenever possible, it's best to clarify our interior landscape before taking action, since it is likely that unless we have first worked with our own negativity, we will make matters worse.

As an example of the predictable pattern of blame, let's say a difficulty arises as the result of feeling criticized. We may immediately feel hurt, which is almost always based in fear. All of the old memories of hurt may come rising out of the cellar, and it's quite possible that the strength of our emotional reaction is based more on the accumulation of past hurts than on the current situation. The beliefs that stem from these accumulated hurts go screaming through our head: "This always happens to me!" "How could she treat me like that?" "See, I knew nobody could be trusted," "I'm so stupid!" or "I can't take this." And we certainly believe these thoughts to be true, especially when we're right in the middle of our reaction. Since it's painful to experience them, we move immediately into avoidance, into our own particular defensive strategy, such as blaming, withdrawing, or seeking diversions.

Whatever our particular defensive pattern is, we have to see that this behavior or strategy, while arising as a means of avoiding feeling the painful quality of our emotional reaction, is not the same as the emotion itself. Furthermore, the only way to actually *feel* the emotion—to say yes to it, to work with and heal it—is to first refrain from the defensive behavioral strategy. Only by refraining from our defensive strategies, particularly the pattern of blaming, can we stay in the present moment of our emotional reactions.

Residing in our emotional reactions most often leads us to the very uncomfortable feeling of fear, which can be the hardest thing of all to stay with. But can you see how fear is a key issue underlying most of our relationship difficulties? Fear, more than anything, is what blocks intimacy and love. These fears may not immediately be apparent, but they're there nonetheless. And they continue to exert a powerful, even overpowering, influence until they're addressed.

But what, exactly, do we fear? Think of your own situation. Can you identify your own particular core fears? Can you see the extent to which these fears drive you, even if you're not feeling them now? In order to practice with difficulties in relationships, it's important to first understand the specific dynamic fear takes within yourself. Some examples include the fears of being abandoned or rejected, of not getting what we want or losing what we have, of intimacy, of being overwhelmed, of losing control or being controlled, of feeling unloved or unworthy, and so on.

These fears are not necessarily logical or reasonable. For example, fearing that we're unworthy of love doesn't mean it's true. It just means that we believe it to be true; consequently, so long as we remain caught in our belief, that fear will control the way we act, react, and relate to others. So first, we have to begin to see clearly our own particular fears, since they underlie almost all of our relationship conflicts.

Then comes the most difficult part of practicing with relationship difficulties—where we have to be willing to be present with, to really *feel* this core quiver of fear-based pain. Knowing our thoughts is important, but this in itself cannot touch our accumulated memory of pain. It's so easy to stay mired in blame, replaying old wounds, but we may eventually find that it's not necessary to stay stuck on the history channel; it's always possible to switch to the discovery channel, where we begin to look at our experience in a new way. The task itself is very straightforward, yet it is nonetheless very difficult to do: we need to refrain from replaying our storyline of drama and blame and instead say yes to the present moment of our experience—to actually feel it, to rest in the bodily sensations no matter how uncomfortable they may be. We might think we can't stand it, but of course we can. We just don't want to.

One practice technique—the Three Breaths Practice—may help when the pain seems too much to bear. We simply tell the ego, which is the source of resistance, that we will only feel the painful feelings for the duration of three breaths. After that, we'll divert ourselves into fantasy or another source of comfort, whatever our form of "chocolate" may be. Then we feel the emotion—that most dreaded thing we haven't wanted to feel—fully and with intention for three breaths. After that, we don't renege on the deal; we allow ourselves to turn away. We do, however, come back to experiencing again and again later, three breaths at a time.

Awareness is what heals. This is the most basic principle of spiritual practice. Awareness is what makes our suffering less solid. As we begin to see through our fears, as they become more porous, they no longer run our behavior, they no longer cause so much pain.

Until we face our fears, we will not be able to truly connect with others, because we'll still be disconnected from ourselves. If we don't become intimate with our own fears, how can we have a healthy relationship with another who is also caught in fear? But as we learn to befriend our fears, we no longer fear them; and when we meet someone who may be angry at us, instead of immediately reacting to the anger, we may understand that they're really just afraid. The path to awakening the heart of compassion toward another is always rooted in our acceptance of our own pain.

Once we become familiar with our own fears, we may find it helpful to communicate them to those who are closest to us. I remember sitting in a restaurant with my wife, Elizabeth, in the first months of our relationship. It was right before a retreat, and for whatever reason, my Pandora's box of fears was wide open. I had never before spoken openly to another person in a detailed way about my fears, mostly out of shame, not wanting to appear weak. But in the prior months of learning to say yes to feeling my fears, I no longer saw them as my enemy or as defeat; so that evening, I chose to tell Elizabeth how I was feeling without holding anything back.

What amazed me was that she simply listened without comment or judgment. It's rare to feel heard, but it's particularly satisfying when we are feeling exposed. The risk we take is being misunderstood, judged, or rejected; but it's worth the risk if our aspiration is to truly connect with another. Honestly sharing our fears is an essential step toward true intimacy in relationships. But in order to do this, we must first be willing to welcome the difficulties that inevitably arise.

This may sound like a somewhat dark and perhaps even bleak view of relationships. You may wish to forget this seemingly grim discussion about saying yes to your pain and fears. You may prefer to focus on the more positive aspects of relationships or think that if something feels bad, the relationship is not healthy. As human beings, we naturally want to lighten up and focus on finding pleasure or comfort in our relationships, but we have to understand that as long as there is suffering in our relationships, we need to bring attention to those areas where we are most stuck.

Through this work, we can come to know the real meaning of love in relationship, no longer settling for superficial security or the comfort of psychological safety. The more we defuse the conditions that we ourselves have imposed on our relationships—the judgments, the perceived wants and needs—the more the path is cleared for love to simply flow through us. Of course, some things will yield more gracefully than others, and we shouldn't be glib about the tremendous challenges we face here.

Practicing Being Kindness

There's an additional step we can take in our work with relationships: practicing Being Kindness toward those we are having difficulty with, as well as toward ourselves. This is, however, a very tricky area, because trying to act from kindness can easily become a moral dictate that bypasses the pain we feel deep inside. For example, if someone is mean to us and we feel hurt, it would not be helpful to try to act kindly in return without *also* addressing what's really going on inside of us. Such kindness would be more cosmetic than real; it's possibly a way to hold on to the image we want to have of ourselves as a kind person. This type of effort is eventually bound to backfire, because it bypasses the underlying anger and fear that prevent us from giving genuine kindness in the first place.

Conversely, when we're willing to acknowledge our own interior and often rocky landscape, making intentional acts of kindness can be very fruitful in that they allow us to face whatever discomfort arises within ourselves from these actions. This is particularly true when we realize that the most difficult thing for us to give to another is often what the other wants most. Think of someone close to you. What does this person want most from you that you're unwilling to give? I'm talking about something you're capable of giving but hold back on out of fear, either a conscious fear or one of which you're not even aware. Take a minute to consider this.

Here's an example: if what our partner wants most from us is acceptance, to act intentionally from kindness would mean that we refrain from criticizing and stop trying to make that person be different from who he or she is. This may sound impossible, or at least very difficult, but consider what's at stake. If we could honestly give nonjudgment to another as an act of kindness, it would force us to work with exactly what we most need to work with—our own fears and attachments around our judgments. Besides, consider how much it might mean to the other to be met with kindness.

We may encounter strong resistance when giving to another what the other wants, particularly if we have been keeping track of grievances for a long time. Still, as we work through the layers of anger, fear, and discomfort underlying our resistance, we'll be freeing ourselves from our own inner barriers. We ordinarily believe that the barriers to love lie in the other person, but these barriers are always our own.

Although we usually assume another person can and should be able to take away our discomfort, this assumption is a major obstruction to experiencing genuine connectedness and love. Working with discomfort is primarily our *own* inner work. Because the practice of giving to another will no doubt highlight our discomfort, doing so allows us to intentionally work with our own pain and fear that are at the root of that discomfort. The practice of giving in this way can thus be our exact path to living from the Being Kindness that is our true nature.

The point is, we don't have to try to feel loving or kind; we just have to work with what gets in the way, particularly where we hold our hearts back in fear. Interestingly, once we work with our own fears, others will often feel the freedom to move toward us. And when others no longer feel the need to defend, they too may become more willing to work with their own stuck places, and we, in turn, will feel more freedom to move toward them.

Memoir of an Unlikely Marriage

ELLEN GRAF

Most relationship experts emphasize the importance of good communication in building lasting relationships. What happens when you don't share a language or a culture with your partner? With humor and insight, Ellen Graf writes about her cross-cultural marriage, inviting us to ponder the aspects of love and relationships that are beyond words.

MY CHINESE FRIEND YILIANG invited herself over for a serious talk. Her English is poor, and she struggled to convey her message, but she was concerned: she had noticed I was lonely. Her brother in China, Zhong-hua, was lonely too. Maybe he and I would like each other? She offered to send me to China to find out. "But if you don't like him, is OK," she said. Her vocabulary exhausted, she drew a huge breath and said, "OK, all done."

I was both stunned by her offer and strangely open to it. At forty-six, I had already been burned to ash by divorce and had slowly come back to life. Three of my four children had grown up and left home. I was looking to meet someone. But I had never considered going to China, and I knew almost nothing about Yiliang's brother.

"What's your brother like?" I asked her the next time we spoke.

"He is very kind, very weak."

"He's very weak? Oh dear."

"Oh dear? I think you don't need 'oh dear.' What does *weak* mean in English?"

"*Weak* means 'not very strong.'"

"No, no. He is not this word, because he is very strong. I cannot translate."

Yiliang's sister-in-law found a few more English words to describe Zhong-hua. Unfortunately, they were the blandest of all: nice and cute. Still, I thought that not choosing for myself might possibly work better for me this time around. Allowing my own attractions to steer my life had only battered my heart.

Four months later, I found myself in the Beijing airport amid a surge of people politely pushing, shuffling, and nudging past one another. This was unlike an American crowd, where you feel harried, even accosted. There, I sailed comfortably through a sea of introverts.

I saw one solid figure standing absolutely still. A multitude pressed and swayed around him. He held red roses, and beads of moisture clung to his resolute jaw. He wore an expression of contained expectancy. The temperature was ninety-nine degrees.

I immediately felt calm in his presence. Our courtship had already occurred in the form of our shared anticipation, though we hadn't communicated, hadn't even exchanged pictures. But his being open to me, sight unseen, meant a lot. We had tried so hard in previous marriages, only to fail. So I traveled to him with an eager heart, and he welcomed me with the same.

During our three weeks together, the absence of spoken words let things be themselves. I felt the air tingling and warm with a companionship sheltered from discourse.

At our first dinner, he placed each delicacy on my plate and watched without making eye contact or smiling. Of the locusts and sea slug, he gave me just a little and nodded once encouragingly to say, "Try." He saw I loved shrimp and piled more onto the plate. Out of necessity, the first phrase I learned in Chinese was "I am full."

When he asked, "Do you want marry?" I said yes. I was surprised, actually, that he could say the words; he must have practiced and practiced. Later we had a simple ceremony, and I returned to the United States to wait eighteen months for him to be granted a visa. During this time, we communicated as best we could by phone and letters. His voice was balm to my nerves, and the monthly rice-paper letters were always from "the brootom" of his heart.

In return, translating with a dictionary, I sometimes wrote characters that had been out of popular use in China for centuries. When I asked after his father, it probably sounded something like, "I prithee, how fareth the honorable ancestor?"

Finally the day arrived when I was waiting at the Albany airport for him. It was winter. As soon as I took him into my house, he deftly made himself at home. At the woodstove, he removed his business pants and stood there in his baggy, quilted long underwear. "Very comfortable," he said, one of the few phrases he knew at the time.

After our meal, he rummaged in the bathroom until he found the mop, bucket, and Murphy Oil Soap. He proceeded to scrub in silence all the floors, upstairs and down. Then he went out on the snowy porch in his black business shoes and long underwear, looked up at the starry sky, and had a smoke.

As is common in China, there were no random smiles, no effort at small talk, no hand squeezing or gentle pats. My husband would no sooner pat my hand or kiss my cheek than pat his own hand or kiss his image in the mirror. I had to feel the air to know if everything was OK or not. I decided it was OK and went to bed, leaving him in the snow. When he came to bed, he held me as if I were something long lost and precious that might not live until morning.

Shortly after arriving, Zhong-hua suggested we sell the refrigerator: "Just two people no need." In China, many people do not own a refrigerator. They shop daily for fresh meat and vegetables and, after a meal, leave leftover food uncovered on the table until it is consumed.

One day, I found four dozen eggs in the cupboard, and Zhong-hua said that was "no problem," because in China eggs are kept unrefrigerated for up to two months. I said the eggs were different here and convinced him to wait on selling the refrigerator. It soon became a hazard. His sister, whom we both now called *Da Jie,* "Big Sister," showed up once a month with poppy-colored plastic bags from the Chinese grocery bursting with Chinese cabbage, bok choy, spinach, and daikon like short baseball bats. She brought cases of mangoes and stacks of eggs six dozen high. Every time the refrigerator door was opened, a Chinese cabbage or two tumbled to the floor and sharp-clawed chicken feet startled me from under bunches of cilantro and watercress. Bags of frozen cuttlefish stacked in the freezer had a way of sliding out like bobsleds and hitting me in the chest.

I had never eaten giant sea slugs or sheep's stomach. I tried them, once. He had never eaten cheese or mashed potatoes. He tried them, once. He tasted small, tentative half-spoonfuls of ice cream. He stirred it vigorously to warm it up and, when that didn't work, poured hot tea over it. We both went hungry or suffered indigestion when the other made supper. We endured this food trauma for six months. He lost fifteen pounds. I lost ten. After that, he still would not touch cheese or homemade chicken potpie but could devour an entire half-gallon of chocolate ice cream in one sitting. He said if food could not be eaten until it was all gone, then it was no good. "One time, eat all gone" was the rule. He was also fond of repeating his father's maxim that a craving is your body telling you what it needs to be healthy.

I still hated slugs but became accustomed to my lips going numb while eating his hot Shandong province cuisine. I enjoyed rock fungus, squid, and what I came to know as "smelly fish." This salted fish, when deep-fried, "Smells very bad, but tastes very good," just as Zhong-hua said. Its smell filled the house with an odor like that of a men's wrestling team locker room. In early spring, Zhong-hua purchased a large package of tripe but was disgusted by how dirty it was, unlike the tripe he could buy in China. Scrubbing the gritty sheets of intestines under running water took more than an hour. While the huge open pot bubbled on the stove, Zhong-hua again reassured me, "Smells very bad but tastes very good."

Later the same day, I was outside hanging laundry when I heard my daughter screech, *"Mom, Mom! The house is on fire!"* I ran up from the garden. Green, foul-smelling smoke poured out of the windows. The electric burner glowed fiery red, and the water had boiled from the pot, leaving smoking cinders of pig's bowels. The house was not on fire, just the tripe. We threw open all the doors and windows. This only chilled the hideous smell without decreasing it.

When Zhong-hua reappeared, he broke his rule of "never say sorry to your wife." "Sorry! Sorry!" he said, grinning, though technically the apology was directed at my daughter. This ban on "sorry" is part of a cultural model that considers it not only unnecessary but inappropriate and offensive to extend certain polite or conciliatory gestures to one's spouse. It is as if doing so identifies him or her as "other." Other forbiddances include "thank you," "hello," "good-bye," "excuse me," and "please." Whenever he used one of these words, he said it as if on stage, with great gusto and enunciation. It struck him as so funny that he burst into uncharacteristic laughter, especially with "excuse me."

He routinely bumped into me in a deliberate manner if I was in his path. The collisions usually happened in the kitchen while we both prepared food. He pushed me along, using his ample stomach as a snowplow until he had enough counter space. I didn't realize that bodily rudeness was a privilege of intimacy, and I made a point of being offended. When I tried to explain the concept of "excuse me," my husband looked at me with impatient disbelief. He said, "This kind of thing in our home no need, because this is *family*. Family no need these kind of words." Understanding that he was operating out of a belief system and not out of rudeness, I tried his way. Pushing him out of the way with a forceful thrust of the hip was fun, though he was very solid and removing him to another location took several tries.

I gradually learned to prepare many Chinese dishes that my husband found edible, if not as hot or salty as he preferred. So I was puzzled why, when friends came over to eat and the conversation turned to food, my husband would rudely disparage my cooking: "Ellen cooks everything not very good. Ellen's sister is good cook, but Ellen not. One time Ellen cooked rice, squash, onion, all mixed together—tastes very, very terrible." He put great emphasis on the *very*.

I was not immediately offended, because I knew that my husband greatly preferred Chinese cuisine. However, my sister cooks American food, so that comparison put a different slant on things. He was insulting me, not American food. He made blunt, unflattering comments about my ability to cook, clean, dance, and practice Tai Chi intended for the ears of outsiders. Eventually, I learned that these negative compliments were intended to discourage jealousy and repel wife-snatchers. It worked very well. The friends were stopped short. They opened their mouths but said nothing. They looked at me sympathetically. I shrugged and smiled to reassure them. "It's a Chinese tradition," I said, "to say your wife is not good at various things." They nodded rapidly, smiling tentatively, not sure if they should be smiling or frowning or how to exit the conversation.

Zhong-hua had trouble finding work. A friend kindly hired him to help on a painting job. Great, I thought. But back home he had been a businessman, and I didn't know that many post-Mao urban Chinese have complicated feelings of shame about performing paid manual labor. He gamely went along, but it was a disaster that ended with the friend pressing $200 into his hand and saying he didn't need a helper the next day.

I also didn't know that as a child, Zhong-hua had endured hard labor far more grueling than house painting. He had worked side by side with village farmers, standing bare-legged in icy water for hours, scooping out silt for fertilizer. His parents, ravaged by poverty and famine, often did little more for him than count his head as he safely returned at night. For his first nineteen years, my husband endured such hardship and deprivation that, by adulthood, he had cultivated an internal equilibrium that was not easily upset.

I had long sought a peace unaffected by the weather outside.

Soon another friend gave him a job at his natural foods store. Zhong-hua had no driver's license, so the owner went miles out of his way to pick him up and take him home at night. But how long would that last? I needed to teach him how to drive. In China, he had driven a motorcycle but not a car. How different could it be?

First of all, the center line had no significance to him. And I had to instruct him that the car on the main road has the right-of-way and a red light means "stop."

Accelerating through an intersection, he said, "I don't think so."

"Yes, that's the law!"

"In China, who can go, just go. Is OK. Big road, small road, left turn, right turn—this doesn't matter. Also, people drive any side of road. Which side open, which side drive."

"What if another car is coming?"

"No problem. Just not hit other car is OK."

"Watch out! That guy is passing you on the right. You should be in the slow lane. Stay in your lane!"

I was gasping and holding on to the ceiling, my feet braced against the dash. He said I must ride in the back, because I was making him nervous and this was "very danger." He pulled over and I got out, took a few deep breaths, and repositioned myself rigidly in the back seat, pressing my mouth shut except to yelp, "Stay in your lane! Do you know what a lane is?"

I wasn't in the habit of drinking alcohol, but for several weeks, upon each safe return, I sedated myself with Chinese wine, the kind that numbs your lips for a full hour.

Barren winter trees allowed our elderly neighbors, Dave and Flippy, to keep a watchful eye on events at our place, and often Dave would telephone to offer assistance: "Hey, I wasn't doing anything and wondered if you want me to bring my tractor up. I can pull that car out of the ditch easy. No sense you two hurting yourselves."

One night, returning home through a blackness laden with spring snowflakes, my husband pulled up to the kitchen door to drop me off. I was so grateful. All that practice was paying off.

He reappeared in the doorway minutes later. "Sorry!" he said and started quaking in silent laughter, looking down and shaking his head.

"Sorry?"

"Yes! Very sorry. You see!" He pulled me out to the garage. I looked in where the car should be, but nothing was there. Then I lifted my eyes and saw the taillights going west through a gaping hole in the garage. I ran around to the back and beheld the front of the car hanging in midair over the stone embankment.

The AAA tow truck came and pulled the car back into the garage, no questions asked. We patched together the garage wall. The next time it happened, a week later, the same AAA driver arrived. "I know what to do, ma'am," he said.

During that first year, we used our full allotment of AAA service calls while Zhong-hua advanced from mistakenly pouring transmission fluid into the crankcase to being able to install alternators, timing belts, electrical components, and an automatic transmission. His method of repair generally requires two days of sitting in front of the problem, thinking and smoking Old Golds, before he touches anything.

But his driving troubles persist. The police trail him. Motorists shake fists at him. He can't remember the rule about not turning left from the right lane and recently put us in the path of a Lincoln zooming up fast. Tires screamed, and soon Zhong-hua was looking into the quivering jowls of the red-faced driver, who jabbed at him with a meaty forefinger, then stuck his face out the window and sputtered, "You almost killed us!"

"Yes."

"I said you almost killed us, buddy. Do you hear?"

"Yes, yes."

"What do you have to say when I say you almost killed us?"

"Thank you very much!"

"I'm yelling at you. Why do you say thank you?"

"I don't know. I just think, thank you."

"OK, you're welcome," the guy said, before warily proceeding.

Zhong-hua waved and thanked him again.

And so it goes. Sometimes I remember our car grinding in slow motion off the gravel shoulder and totaling itself benignly against a rotten tree stump. I see us climbing out of the tilting wreckage, distraught but unhurt, and wonder if we were gently nudged off the road and thus saved from some other horrible highway fate.

Somebody must be looking out for us. A few years ago, my life was roadworthy but lonely—it cried out for an intervention. Now every day feels like a wild car ride with Zhong-hua: lurching and unpredictable, but rich with humor, determination, and devotion.

I don't question it. Like my husband, I just think, "Thank you."

Present Moment Listening

ARTHUR JEON

When you listen to your partner—without prejudgment or opinion—this frees you up to become truly present for them. Yoga and meditation teacher Arthur Jeon addresses what it means to give the gift of your undivided attention.

MOST COUPLES who have been together for a long time point to communication as an important ingredient in their relationships, if not *the* most important. But what exactly does good communication mean? Does it mean you can say anything to your partner? Or does it mean that you never want to say the thing that can't be unsaid?

One of the ways in which you can take the stars from your eyes and really see another person is to simply listen to them, to give them the gift of your full, undivided attention without judgment or agenda. Don't be thinking about how you might be able to help them or what you're going to say when they stop talking. Be receptive but not passive. Actively listen without being aware of being a "listener."

What does this mean? It means that you are not looking at your partner and thinking that what he's saying is right or wrong, true or untrue, good or bad. It simply *is*. Listen as though you're just trying to understand what the other person is saying. Literally be like a reporter trying to get the facts of what the other person is trying to communicate, without prejudgment or opinion. This frees you up to become totally present for your partner.

I can hear some of you saying that that's impossible. How can you listen without forming an opinion, argument, or rebuttal? To which I would say that it's impossible to truly listen while thinking. So listening without any reference back to "me" or "my thoughts"—listening without any sense of "I" is the only way in which you can truly listen as opposed to simply hearing.

Many problems in a relationship result from a back-and-forth, he said/she said power struggle. The focus is on trying to convince or change your partner or trying to make the other person wrong and make you right. But think about it for a moment. If you have successfully made somebody "wrong," how are they going to feel? When you make somebody wrong, they will hold resentment and will wait, perhaps unconsciously, to make you wrong. And so goes the endless power struggle that eliminates any chance of peace in the relationship. As soon as you insert the "I think" into the process of listening, you are out of the moment.

Men often make the mistake of trying to solve the problems of their partner. It's a natural impulse for us. We are "doers." But often what women want is simply to give voice to what is bothering them, to be heard. I am a yoga and meditation teacher, and one day as I was coming out of teaching a yoga class, I met Clara, one of my students, walking out of the parking lot.

"How are you?" I asked as we fell into step with each other.

"Oh, you know. Just having one of those days. Know what I mean? Just not feeling right."

"Yes, that can happen," I said. We approached the top of the staircase. I glanced at her face and saw a state that I recognized. Clara's pretty face was plagued by thoughts. Suffering from the nonstop nattering of her mind, she couldn't wake up into the moment. As we stood at the top of the stairs, I recognized the suffering state, having been there myself, and I thought I could help.

"Do you want to change your mood by the time we reach the bottom of the stairs?" I asked the question lightly, not wanting to push her. I had in mind a simple mindfulness exercise, one in which each step you take becomes a call to wakefulness in the present moment. With each step down, you focus your awareness in the *now,* using the staircase as a metaphor for descending out of the "small self" of nonstop thought into the larger self of universal consciousness. It's a simple exercise, always available to you, no matter what you are doing. By focusing your attention on the task at hand, by allowing yourself to be absorbed in the moment with what is happening, no matter what it is, the mind's madness gets crowded out by the vibrancy of now.

Clara was having none of it.

"No, that's okay. I'm fine."

"Oh. Okay," I said, surprised.

"See you later." She stepped quickly down the stairs and disappeared out the door.

Instead of simply listening, I'd gone into "teacher" mode. I tried to fix her problem. But all Clara needed was a sympathetic ear, a "Yes, I hear you; some days are like that." That would have been the most empathic response.

Now comes the tricky part of this. Even if you know you're right, even if you can see that another person's suffering is being caused by them, even if you know how you can truly help them, most of the time the wiser path is simply to listen. If they want advice, they will ask for it.

This is just one way in which it is better just to listen to somebody who is trying to communicate with you.

Become listening but not a *listener*. Become invisible to yourself.

In this way, you can really show up for your partner in the present moment.

PART FOUR

Dealing with Difficulties

Those Aren't Fighting Words, Dear

LAURA MUNSON

When memoirist Laura Munson's husband said he wanted a divorce, she didn't issue ultimatums, yell, cry, or beg. Instead, she gave him space and took responsibility for her own happiness. This isn't the divorce story you think it is.

LET'S SAY YOU HAVE what you believe to be a healthy marriage. You're still friends and lovers after spending more than half of your lives together. The dreams you set out to achieve in your twenties—gazing into each other's eyes in candlelit city bistros when you were single and skinny—have for the most part come true.

Two decades later, you have the twenty acres of land, the farmhouse, the children, the dogs and horses. You're the parents you said you would be, full of love and guidance. You've done it all: Disneyland, camping, Hawaii, Mexico, city living, stargazing.

Sure, you have your marital issues, but on the whole, you feel so self-satisfied about how things have worked out that you would never, in your wildest nightmares, think you would hear these words from your husband one fine summer day: "I don't love you anymore. I'm not sure I ever did. I'm moving out. The kids will understand. They'll want me to be happy."

But wait. This isn't the divorce story you think it is. Neither is it a begging-him-to-stay story. It's a story about hearing your husband say, "I don't love you anymore," and deciding not to believe him. And what can happen as a result.

Here's a visual: Child throws a temper tantrum. Tries to hit his mother. But the mother doesn't hit back, lecture, or punish. Instead, she ducks. Then she tries to go about her business as if the tantrum isn't happening. She doesn't "reward" the tantrum. She simply doesn't take the tantrum personally because, after all, it's not about her.

Let me be clear: I'm not saying my husband was throwing a child's tantrum. No. He was in the grip of something else—a profound and far more troubling meltdown that comes not in childhood but in midlife, when we perceive that our personal trajectory is no longer arcing reliably upward as it once did. But I decided to respond the same way I'd responded to my children's tantrums. And I kept responding to it that way. For four months.

"I don't love you anymore. I'm not sure I ever did."

His words came at me like a speeding fist, like a sucker punch, yet somehow in that moment, I was able to duck. And once I recovered and composed myself, I managed to say, "I don't buy it." Because I didn't.

He drew back in surprise. Apparently he'd expected me to burst into tears, to rage at him, to threaten him with a custody battle. Or beg him to change his mind.

So he turned mean. "I don't like what you've become."

Gut-wrenching pause. How could he say such a thing? That's when I really wanted to fight. To rage. To cry. But I didn't.

Instead, a shroud of calm enveloped me, and I repeated those words, "I don't buy it."

You see, I'd recently committed to a nonnegotiable understanding with myself. I'd committed to "The End of Suffering." I'd finally managed to exile the voices in my head that told me my personal happiness was only as good as my outward success, rooted in things that were often outside my control. I'd seen the insanity of that equation and decided to take responsibility for my own happiness. And I mean all of it.

My husband hadn't yet come to this understanding with himself. He had enjoyed many years of hard work, and its rewards had supported our family of four all along. But his new endeavor hadn't been going so well, and his ability to be the breadwinner was in rapid decline. He'd been miserable about this, felt useless, was losing himself emotionally and letting himself go physically. And now he wanted out of our marriage, to be done with our family.

But I wasn't buying it.

I said, "It's not age-appropriate to expect children to be concerned with their parents' happiness. Not unless you want to create codependents who'll spend their lives in bad relationships and therapy. There are times in every relationship when the parties involved need a break. What can we do to give you the distance you need without hurting the family?"

"Huh?" he said.

"Go trekking in Nepal. Build a yurt in the back meadow. Turn the garage studio into a man-cave. Get that drum set you've always wanted. Anything but hurting the children and me with a reckless move like the one you're talking about."

Then I repeated my line, "What can we do to give you the distance you need without hurting the family?"

"Huh?"

"How can we have a responsible distance?"

"I don't want distance," he said. "I want to move out."

My mind raced. Was it another woman? Drugs? Unconscionable secrets? But I stopped myself. I would not suffer.

Instead, I went to my desk, Googled "responsible separation," and came up with a list. It included things like: Who's allowed to use what credit cards? Who are the children allowed to see you with in town? Who's allowed keys to what?

I looked through the list and passed it on to him.

His response: "Keys? We don't even have keys to our house."

I remained stoic. I could see pain in his eyes. Pain I recognized.

"Oh, I see what you're doing," he said. "You're going to make me go into therapy. You're not going to let me move out. You're going to use the kids against me."

"I never said that. I just asked, what can we do to give you the distance you need?"

"Stop saying that!"

Well, he didn't move out.

Instead, he spent the summer being unreliable. He stopped coming home at his usual six o'clock. He would stay out late and not call. He blew off our entire Fourth of July—the parade, the barbecue, the fireworks—to go to someone else's party. When he was at home, he was distant. He wouldn't look me in the eye. He didn't even wish me happy birthday.

But I didn't play into it. I walked my line. I told the kids, "Daddy's having a hard time as adults often do. But we're a family, no matter what." I was not going to suffer. And neither were they.

My trusted friends were irate on my behalf. "How can you just stand by and accept this behavior? Kick him out! Get a lawyer!"

I walked my line with them too. This man was hurting, yet his problem wasn't mine to solve. In fact, I needed to get out of his way so he could solve it.

I know what you're thinking: I'm a pushover. I'm weak and scared and would put up with anything to keep the family together. I'm probably one of those women who would endure physical abuse. But I can assure you, I'm not. I load 1,500-pound horses into trailers and gallop through the high country of Montana all summer. I went through Pitocin-induced natural childbirth. And a cesarean section without follow-up drugs. I am handy with a chain saw.

I simply had come to understand that I was not at the root of my husband's problem. He was. If he could turn his problem into a marital fight, he could make it about us. I needed to get out of the way so that wouldn't happen.

Privately, I decided to give him time. Six months.

I had good days, and I had bad days. On the good days, I took the high road. I ignored his lashing out, his merciless jabs. On bad days, I would fester in the August sun while the kids ran through sprinklers, raging at him in my mind. But I never wavered. Although it may sound ridiculous to say, "Don't take it personally," when your husband tells you he no longer loves you, sometimes that's exactly what you have to do.

Instead of issuing ultimatums, yelling, crying, or begging, I presented him with options. I created a summer of fun for our family and welcomed him to share in it or not—it was up to him. If he chose not to come along, we would miss him, but we would be just fine, thank you very much. And we were.

And, yeah, you can bet I wanted to sit him down and persuade him to stay. To love me. To fight for what we've created. You can bet I wanted to.

But I didn't.

I barbecued. Made lemonade. Set the table for four. Loved him from afar.

And one day, there he was, home from work early, mowing the lawn. A man doesn't mow his lawn if he's going to leave it. Not this man. Then he fixed a door that had been broken for eight years. He made a comment about our front porch needing paint. Our front porch. He mentioned needing wood for next winter. The future. Little by little, he started talking about the future.

It was Thanksgiving dinner that sealed it. My husband bowed his head humbly and said, "I'm thankful for my family."

He was back.

And I saw what had been missing: pride. He'd lost pride in himself. Maybe that's what happens when our egos take a hit in midlife and we realize we're not as young and golden anymore. When life's knocked us around. And our childhood myths reveal themselves to be just that. The truth feels like the biggest sucker punch of them all: it's not a spouse or land or a job or money that brings us happiness. Those achievements, those relationships, can enhance our happiness, yes, but happiness has to start from within. Relying on any other equation can be lethal.

My husband had become lost in the myth. But he found his way out. We've since had the hard conversations. In fact, he encouraged me to write about our ordeal. To help other couples who arrive at this juncture in life. People who feel scared and stuck. Who believe their temporary feelings are permanent. Who see an easy out and think they can escape.

My husband tried to strike a deal. Blame me for his pain. Unload his feelings of personal disgrace onto me.

But I ducked. And I waited. And it worked.

It Used to Be So Exciting

BRENDA SHOSHANNA

The first kiss was electric; the first three months were a dream. But boredom has set in, and now, according to psychologist Brenda Shoshanna, we have a choice. We can slip out the back door, or we can learn why ordinary love is so very precious.

EMILY, THIRTY-TWO, had been seeing Dave, who is forty, for four years. Their relationship was comfortable and had fallen into an expected pattern of routines. They'd visit his family for Thanksgiving, her family for Christmas. They went to the same restaurants for dinner and took the same two-week vacation every April in the Caribbean. Emily wondered if she had already experienced what life would be like with Dave, if there could ever be anything new and exciting in their relationship. She occasionally caught herself looking at younger men, fantasizing about exciting, different encounters, and wondered if she could deal with the monotony of being with Dave forever. On the other hand, she didn't know if she should just cut it all off and have wasted the past four years of her life.

It could be said that Emily was staying with Dave for practical reasons, largely based on her desire for security and fear of losing valuable time. But her desire for other men indicates a yearning for the excitement she no longer found or allowed herself to have with Dave. Enmeshed in the secure routine she had established, Emily had not gone deeper in her experience of what it means to truly love. By leaving one partner for another, excitement and thrills may increase temporarily, but ultimately this pattern leads nowhere, except to an addiction to being excited and developing a need for constant change.

As Emily's anguish about her relationship with Dave deepened, she started to practice Zen meditation. She decided to attend a *sesshin*, an intensive meditation retreat, hoping that this would bring about a radical change.

"I'm going because I can't change. I can't make a move in the relationship," she said. "Also, I can't wait for something to happen anymore. I've had it with waiting." Emily felt that she would speed things up by going away for the week.

After she got to her retreat and became oriented to what the week would be like, she breathed deeply, initially relieved. Every day, there would be numerous thirty- to fifty-minute meditation sessions interspersed with meals and mindful periods of work. She felt certain this week would provide a turning point for the rest of her life. She would not come home the same person. She would be able to leave Dave on the spot.

We all have huge expectations that we expect to be fulfilled when we do something new. When we enter new relationships, we usually place these expectations on the new relationship as well.

By the end of the first day of the meditation retreat, Emily was exhausted, bored, achy, and sad. Her legs hurt, and her back was stiff. She couldn't believe that she would have to go through this same routine for seven days on end. She hadn't fully realized when she signed up what she was getting into.

None of us realize what we're getting into when we sign on for a relationship either. At first, it looks glamorous and exciting. Then the inexorable reality of everyday life begins to set in. Emily had no idea how she would get through a whole week. She wanted to talk it over with someone, but unless there was an emergency, unless someone was sick or needed something specific, talking was forbidden. She could not resolve her difficulty here by spilling it out on another.

Other people looked as though they were doing fine, Emily thought as she looked around. Was it only she who felt so irritated? She didn't have much time to ponder, as lights were shut off half an hour after the schedule ended for the day. She lay there in her bed, tossing, desperately trying to fall asleep. She'd have to be up at four-thirty the next morning.

By the middle of the second day, Emily felt lonely and angry. When the meals were served, she refused her food. That will let them know something's wrong, Emily thought, trying to get attention of some kind. The student who served the food just passed her by, however, serving the person next to her. She was the one who would be hungry, she realized, if she did not take what was offered when it came. In like manner, she was the one who would stay miserable if, all through the retreat, she was determined to focus upon her own personal agenda rather than focus upon her breath, which came and went regardless of everything, bringing new life each moment and taking old hurts away. But Emily just sat there thinking how she could get away.

By the end of the third day, Emily, unwilling to give up her thoughts and fantasies, decided to run away. There was no way she was going to continue like this. Day after day, the same things happened. There was no change or release. She felt as if the whole world were on her shoulders. There was no one to help or to talk to. Except for brief meetings with the teacher, which were only about her meditation practice, she could not turn to anyone else. She had hoped this sesshin would expedite her life, that she would be through with waiting, but here there was nothing but waiting itself. She sat there waiting for the sitting to end, desperate for the bell that signals the end of the practice period to ring out.

In a sense, an intensive meditation retreat is like a microscope, intensifying and enlarging both our way of functioning and the issues we are dealing with. As the days go by, it becomes impossible not to see who we are and what we are up against. Hiding in denial and fantasy is no longer possible.

Emily's sense of what it meant to be fully alive was built upon change, excitement, and rejection of boredom and of the daily routine. In retreat, in order to survive, she had to completely enter into and embrace the routine itself. She had to forget about her personal agenda and be fully in each moment as it came. That was the only way for time to pass easily. That was the only way to discover moments of beauty and joy.

At the end of the third day, Emily packed her bags just before the lights went out. Then when it was dark, she went out the back door to her car, which was parked on a hill, and ran away.

Once on the road home, a sense of loss and failure encircled her, a sense of not having gone through what was needed and having deserted the person sitting next to her in the meditation hall. As Emily drove a little farther, she realized there was nowhere she could really run.

Then, in the middle of the night on a country road, she turned her car around and drove back in time to be at sesshin for the early-morning sitting. Except for one student, who looked at her oddly the next day at breakfast, she didn't think anyone even realized that she had gone and returned.

At some point in the sesshin, almost all students feel they cannot go on. But no matter what happens, they go forward with their scheduled activities, remaining mindful through them, no matter how they feel. This itself is an enormous lesson, both in sesshin and in relationships. No matter how we feel, we do not act impulsively. We do not let our feelings dictate the next step to take. We just put one foot in front of the other and continue doing what needs to be done. We do not dwell upon our upset either or assign some special meaning to it. If we do, it becomes hard to continue.

As the days go by, we cannot help but see that waves of feelings come and go, much like high and low tide at the seashore. Instead of getting pulled offshore by our passing fantasies and feelings, we simply return our attention to what we are doing, where the next step is taking us. As we do so over and over, the storms fade away, and it becomes easier to see clearly.

Of course, there are those who run away from sesshin, just as there are those who run away from their lives (and relationships). As they pack up and slip out the back door, there may even be an initial sense of elation, jubilation. Out of there, finally! They may jump in their car and drive it at breakneck speed down the hill, but then they suddenly realize there is nowhere they can really run. Wherever they go, they take themselves along.

Leaving is hard to do. Returning is even harder. Some do not return because they cannot face the shame of having left. But once an individual is able to return to a sesshin (or relationship), there is the possibility of her making it her very own, fully appreciating its value and gaining some humility along the way. Some punish themselves for leaving. But the true focus should be upon the wonder and strength needed to come back again.

We return when we realize that there is nowhere to run to, that we must learn patience, persistence, and the beauty of life's ordinary routines. We are then ready to understand relationships, the sameness we have to face with our partner day in and day out. Then we are ready to break through the veneer of boredom and find out what it means to really love.

The Hidden Treasure of Anger

Polly Young-Eisendrath

Your throat is contracting, your fists are clenching—but don't deny your anger, says psychologist Polly Young-Eisendrath. Instead, learn to mine it for new ways to work with yourself and the person you love.

IN MANY WAYS, human anger is a treasure. The Greeks called it the "moral emotion," because they noted that animals did not possess it; animals, the Greeks observed, got aggressive and showed fight-or-flight reactivity. They did not get angry. Humans, on the other hand, could experience and express anger with its inherent reflective component: "I can see/know/feel that someone or something has wronged me."

As a response to being wronged, anger is a boundary setter that says, "Stop! I can't tolerate this," or "This isn't working for me." It is not blaming the other or shaming the self. Often experienced first as a contraction in the throat, chest, stomach, or abdomen and a clenching of the fist, anger may be associated with the words "I can't go on like this" seared into the mind.

Anger—sparked by injustice—is at the root of all protest movements, all major processes of change. In our most intimate relationships, when we or our loved ones experience or express anger, it is an opportunity to get to know one another better, to get closer and clearer, and to work with ourselves in a new way. It is an opportunity to ask ourselves, "Why am I feeling this?" "What needs to change here?" and "What do I need to do about it?"

Because anger is expressed at a moment of need, the person expressing it is vulnerable. If, when our partner is angry, we inquire into his need to be seen, treated, known, or held more wholly, dearly, or fairly, we have a chance of accepting our beloved more fully. In our closest relationships, our fate is bound up with the fate of the other. In Buddhist terms, our karma is interwoven, and we cannot easily escape feeling the consequences of the beloved's actions. It is a natural desire for us to want to keep our partner safe or happy, for both selfish and unselfish reasons. But, as a result, we have a tendency to want to control our beloved—and that often creates a sense of being unfairly treated.

Our closest relationships are the most challenging in our lives when it comes to practicing fairness, equality, and kindness. That is because in these intimate relationships we always begin to get to know the other person (even if that person is an infant) through a process of psychological projection: seeing/feeling/experiencing the other through already familiar views, desires, and ideals. This is especially true in romantic love, where we "fall" in love through an idealizing projection and assume that the other is ideal for us and meets our needs in some particular or general way. When the other person does not do or become what we want, which is always the case, we can easily turn against him with hatred, rejection, or pain. Working with anger skillfully can actually be very helpful in our not doing this.

Anger has unfortunately been confused or conflated with aggression, hatred, or rage—some of its more destructive siblings. Many people make the mistake of pushing away anger, being afraid that it will be destructive if expressed. Some may hypervalue silence as though it were its own virtue. Others may express aggression, blame, anxiety, or rage instead of anger. But if you have the skill to feel your feelings with a gentle acceptance of them, you are less likely to dissociate from your feelings or distance yourself from another in times of anger. You won't have to hide your anger from yourself, and you can learn about speaking it honestly and kindly—and about inquiring into your beloved's anger at you.

Knowing what anger really is, we can appreciate how it allows us to avoid destructive behavior, such as fighting or diminishing others and ourselves. The next time our partner does something we don't like or the next time she approaches us saying, "I feel overlooked or unfairly treated," we can begin a process of inquiry that leads to the possibility of accepting differences or changing our actions without blaming the other or having a sense of being blamed.

In order to do this, we need a little wisdom and a few mindfulness skills. To begin, we must remember the first noble truth: life is filled with stress and unsatisfactoriness that are not the fault of anyone in particular. Misunderstandings and oversights are simply part of the muddle of human affairs, especially when we live together on a daily basis and have lots of different needs and perspectives. So when faced with anger—our own or another's—it's a good idea to start with a bit of modesty.

We can then make a commitment to watch our own feelings. We will notice how they arise and pass away, no matter how painful or contractive they are, and that we experience them as body sensations, internal images, and internal talk. Over time, we will become familiar with the emotional landscape of anger. My own anger arises with my chest tightening and my throat constricting, and it tends to shape into the inner words "I can't stand this," or something similar. I label it "anger" fairly quickly. Then I am interested in discovering just what it is that seems unfair to me at that moment. The sense of being treated unfairly should not be overlooked or brushed aside. We will learn from answering the questions "Why am I feeling this?" "What needs to change here?" and "What do I need to do about it?"

Once we see how our feelings arise and pass away on their own, without our doing anything in particular, then we have true freedom to decide when and if we want to express our feelings in words to another. Of course, even if we don't express ourselves in words directly, the other person may read our emotion accurately and may choose to question us about it. Knowing how and when it is useful to express our feelings, especially anger, means paying close attention to the consequences of our speech. Often, anger is an important motivator to talk about what is bothering us, but we first have to reflect. What happens when we speak anger? What happens when we don't? Is it possible to speak anger honestly and kindly at the same time? (Yes, it is, but you have to find your own way each time.)

Equanimity, or gentle, matter-of-fact attention to all of our experiences helps us work with our own and another's anger. Equanimity means to have an open and relaxed view of what's happening while getting our "sea legs," our balance in the midst of being tumbled around. If you can maintain equanimity in the face of your own and your beloved's anger, then you'll be able to feel your own feelings and listen to your beloved at the same time. By slowing down your reactivity, you'll be able to think about the potential consequences of speaking or not speaking in any given moment.

But beware of trying to do all this in a "perfect" way. You cannot get good at delving into the treasure of anger without making mistakes. If you speak out in an aggressive, blaming manner, you can apologize! You can hear yourself speak and say, "I'm sorry. I don't like what I said there. Let me try again, because I love you and I want to understand what is going on." Similarly, if you defend yourself in a preemptive way and walk away from an angry partner, you can turn around and go back. Apologize. Remember: there is no perfect way to do this; there is only the intention to do it and the attempt to follow that intention.

What is the most skillful intention in relation to anger? In my view, it's being interested in anger—your own and another's. True anger is about unfairness, injustice, and intolerable treatment. Inquiring into the source of anger and trying to understand its message is very useful. Using skillful speech is very helpful: use "I" statements rather than talking about what the other person is doing to you, and speak descriptively about the problem. For example, "It doesn't work for me when you walk away while I am in the middle of telling you about my difficult day at work, as you did or seemed to do this morning. I want to talk with you about the thoughts and feelings and questions your behavior triggered in me. Okay?"

The most skillful response to this statement would be, "Please tell me about what you experienced and what you thought was going on." Both of these statements have a tentative tone (a sort of "help me understand what is going on here" tone). At the point that the listener fully understands the speaker (she can check through reflective listening), the listener can then respond with her experience of the event. Frequently, in an intimate relationship, various levels of misunderstanding and misperception are at the source of anger. The process of discovering this usually brings the two people closer. They come to see and know each other more completely, even if the source of the difficulty is not fully resolved.

When you're feeling angry, especially in a close relationship, it's a good time to practice mindfulness and equanimity, not to dissolve the anger but to become more skillful in mining it. See if you can find ways to speak your anger in words that are both honest and kind; stick to "I" statements and stay away from blaming, recalling that blame is a "fight" reaction, not true human anger. The path of love is a difficult one, in large part because of our natural desire to control the beloved. Anger will loosen that sense of control as we come to know our beloved more fully in times of vulnerability. Love and partnership are trainings in the transformation of suffering into compassion and kindness. They teach us the deep lessons of the first noble truth, and they do it in a way that is truly ego-dissolving.

The Green-Eyed Monster

GERI LARKIN

Author and Zen teacher Geri Larkin discusses the dangerous effects of jealousy and its surprisingly simple antidote.

JEALOUSY. Someone takes an interest in our lover, and boom, there it is. Different from envy, where what we have just doesn't measure up to what someone else has, jealousy hits when something we have is threatened or lost to another person. The greater the threat, the bigger the jealousy.

It settles inside of us in stages. At first, we have a feeling that something or someone is moving in on our partner. The more attractive, smart, and wealthy our competitor is, the more threatened we are. In the second stage, we start to obsess. We look for clues that something is going on. (She did touch his arm while they were talking.) Stage three? Our emotions kick in big time. Maybe we start feeling clingy, even though we swore before every god we could name that that would never happen. Not us. Depression is a danger.

We are hurt, angry, jealous. The monster has us.

Moving through jealousy is hard work because, at its worst, it makes us totally crazy. We can think of nothing else; we take obsession to new heights. We could kill. Sometimes we do. Crime statisticians estimate that as many as 35 percent of all murders are the actions of jealous lovers. Sometimes the murder takes the form of suicide. A friend of mine who is a therapist tells me that she can't get through a day without at least one client showing up consumed with jealousy. We want to have our lover, our mate, all to ourselves. And when we don't feel like we do, we're threatened down to our bones. And scared. And mad. A dangerous combination.

Left to its own devices, jealousy grows. Insecurity feeds it, as does any gap in our self-esteem. Maybe another man or woman has appeared on our daily landscape, a new colleague or classmate. My first real bout with jealousy was triggered by a next-door neighbor, a single woman, who started to show up just before dinnertime a couple of times a week. That she was attractive, smart, and funny made my "this could be a threat" antenna stand at full attention.

We find ourselves constantly assessing possible threats when we get stuck in jealousy. We analyze minutia. Does my husband chat with his female colleagues a little too long? Was he looking for an excuse to go over there? Is my partner staying at work longer and longer for no obvious reason? Is she taking longer to get dressed in the morning? And what's with the new lipstick? Sleep deteriorates because we're lying awake trying to figure things out, and the more sleep we lose, the worse things look.

Lodged in jealousy, our emotions run rampant. We're hurt but may not be able to explain why, since we have no proof of wrongdoing (yet). We're ashamed of ourselves. Maybe we become clingy or feel rage. Maybe we become morbidly curious about the person threatening our relationship. Depression kicks in for many of us, as if just being jealous weren't bad enough. In short, we're miserable. At that point, all kinds of things can go wrong.

MINDFULNESS AND JEALOUSY

Mindfulness is about paying attention to what is right smack in front of us. It is a spiritual practice, as well as a realistic method for reducing stress. Mindfulness means slowing down and breathing deeply and noticing your surroundings, as opposed to living your life as though you're looking out the window of a fast-moving bus. When I am being mindful, I notice that the seat of my chair has a black vinyl cushion and the floor is hardwood. I notice how the owners of the coffee shop where I'm sitting matched the tabletops to the floor and how they take time to keep their plants healthy. I notice that the shape of the cup I'm holding is more square than round, that I can't quite call it yellow because there's a little brown in it. In mindfulness, I notice that the wall beside me has little nails sticking out of it—

maybe to hang pictures—and that the shop's Open sign is actually blue and red, not purple like someone told me. I can feel my heart beating and the shape of my favorite black Pilot Precise pen. In this place, paying attention to all of my senses protects me from getting caught up in negative emotions. There's no room.

Instead, I get to watch my emotions come and go, come and go. In a place of mindfulness, I can zoom in on right now instead of getting too caught up in yesterday or tomorrow. The feeling is sweet. Comforting. A refuge.

In this place of true attention, it is impossible to lie to ourselves. What we feel is what we feel. As one result, the light of true attention makes for constant little miracles, because it somehow breaks big chunks of emotions into bite-sized pieces we can ingest and digest—and jealousy is one of those emotions. Without mindfulness, jealousy tends to be big, dark sludge. It makes us tired, miserable, hate-filled. And it is sticky, so when we get caught up in jealousy, it is tough to get uncaught. Instead, we sink deeper and deeper as it hardens, until something explodes. The explosion further fuels our righteousness and misery. Giving in to it makes us feel worse about ourselves, and even after we brush ourselves off after an explosion, there jealousy is, staring at us, daring us to try something else.

Mindfulness breaks the pattern. Why? Because with mindfulness we can see that our jealousy is really made up of lots of other emotions—fear, anger, hurt, sadness, loneliness, embarrassment. Once we see the other emotions, we can work with them individually until jealousy becomes a small thorn in our side instead of an emotional fever come to run us over.

When my son's father and I parted ways, it wasn't because one of us had committed any heinous, relationship-ripping crime. We had moved from Oregon to the University of Michigan together to get our doctorates. Because I was a city-loving woman and he was a mountain man, we agreed to live in Ann Arbor until we both finished our graduate coursework, and then we'd move to a place where he could be in the mountains within a couple of hours at the most and I could get the *New York Times* on Sunday. In those days, Portland, Oregon, didn't get the *Times*.

By the end of our first semester, my husband was ready to head back to the Northwest. The University of Michigan was unbearably competitive, and it didn't help when another student in the program stole a major paper my husband had written and handed it in under his name. By the first thaw, he was at the end of his rope. Was I going with him?

Terrified that I would end up isolated in the mountains making quilts, I refused. Worse, I felt betrayed. We had made a deal.

Brokenhearted, we separated. I stayed in Ann Arbor. As long as we were both single, we stayed close. We talked on the phone, visited. He helped me find an apartment. I was fine when he had the obligatory affair with a much younger woman. When my Portland friends called in to report it, they described her as a younger version of me. I knew her. Since she was smart and beautiful, and he and I were still in contact quite a bit, I was (mostly) happy for him. But their affair ended, and after a few more short flings, he fell in love. Hard. This time it was with a drop-dead gorgeous newscaster—funny, smart, sexy. Did I say thin?

I was jealous. I was stay-up-all-night-and-obsess-about-it jealous. Do-my-best-not-to-wish-her-ill-but-check-the-news-on-the-chance-she-might-be-gone jealous. Even hearing her name riled me. And when I called his house in the mornings (I know, I know) and she answered the phone, my brain went ballistic.

Until she invited me to lunch when I was visiting Portland.

Shocked and, okay, curious, I went. The restaurant was a beautiful garden café, and she was equal to the place. Without waiting for us to order, she told me she'd like to be my friend. Said she could feel a tension from me (no kidding) and wanted to make sure I was okay with their relationship. Stunned, I found myself liking her and even hoping that their relationship would work out.

That afternoon, though, jealousy reared its predictably ugly head.

This time, I sat with it mindfully, motivated to get rid of it. Instead of just labeling what I was feeling—jealousy—I watched to see what was really there and found a bouquet of emotions. First, I was ashamed of myself for giving up a good man for what increasingly felt like a frivolous reason. I felt dowdy compared to the newswoman—and boring. Stupid, even. Watching the emotions come and go for a while, I realized that if I paid attention to them without dwelling on them, they came and went like waves on an ocean. Here one second. Then gone. And they changed shape, got smaller.

After a while, it became clear that what I had been calling jealousy was really sadness. And that I just needed to be sad—that I still had plenty to offer a relationship. After only a week of mindfulness practice regarding my reaction to the lunch, I decided that while I couldn't be her friend, I could honestly wish the two of them happiness and move on. So I did.

Decide What Really Matters

In addition to mindfulness, reframing the things that matter in our lives helps us to move past jealousy. Years ago, I worked as a management consultant. Early on, I became involved with the business plan for a women's magazine. It was a great project. I loved the client. The problem was that the start-up costs of the magazine were so high that I just couldn't make the numbers work. I couldn't figure out how the client could ever make any money. She was furious. I was miserable. I lost her to another firm that apparently could figure out a way for her to make money. Then I was miserable and jealous. After losing an entire day to self-flagellation, I called an older woman, someone who had been a partner in the firm for years. Her advice was blunt.

"Did you do the best you could?"

"Yes."

"Did you apologize for any unskillfulness or mistakes?"

"Yes."

"Will this matter in five years?"

"No."

"Then stop thinking about it."

Relative to everything else in my life, the loss of the client was a disappointment, but that was all. It wasn't like hearing that my child or my parents had been harmed.

Reframing. Last night, I spent some time sitting with a young woman dying from complications related to AIDS. She's in her early twenties—tall, athletic, went to Ivy League schools. She got the disease from a man who raped her at the age of nine. She may not make it to next Christmas. Right now, all she wants is enough energy to make it through two art classes so she can die without any loose ends.

What really matters in our lives?

Jealousy is self-indulgent. It gives us something to obsess about, and with that obsession, it gives meaning to our lives—we have a relationship to defend. Yes, an enemy is at the gate, but too many of us take jealousy to heights that only waste hours, days, months, even years in lives that are already too short.

My Marital Status

James Kullander

James Kullander, a program developer and editor at Omega Institute, had had problems with his wife, Wanda—so much so that they divorced. But then Wanda got sick. Whatever the difficulties, there is only one thing that's real, one thing that lasts: the love between people.

Six years after the event, I still cannot say for sure whether I am divorced or widowed. The question comes up whenever I am filling out a form that wants to know my marital status. All the other questions I can answer in seconds, but this one—which asks that I check *single, married, separated, divorced,* or *widowed*—always stumps me. I'll pause there at the dentist's office, insurance company, or bank, and while the clock ticks and other people's children scamper at my feet, I'll reflect on what it really means to be married.

The event I refer to is the death of the woman who used to be my wife. Wanda was not my wife when she died in December 2001 at the age of forty-two. Not legally, anyway. She and I had met in the summer of 1980, married in the summer of 1984, and divorced in the summer of 1994. Before we'd gotten married, I'd made it clear to Wanda that I did not want children, and she'd told me that she could accept this. Yet, throughout our years together, it seemed she never put her longing to rest. I watched her study the infants our friends and family brought into the world, as if silently hoping I would change my mind. I didn't. I couldn't see the sense in my becoming a parent and said so. Wanda's mother, with her affable prod-dings, would ask me why I'd married her daughter if we weren't going to have children. That, she would say, did not make sense to her.

The discontent Wanda and I felt about each other's intractable posi-tions eventually spread into the rest of our marriage and soured it. What Wanda's mother kept saying began to make sense to me: why stay married if I wasn't going to give Wanda the child she wanted? I was forty; Wanda was thirty-four—still plenty of time for her to have a child with someone else. I talked to Wanda about it, we put ourselves through a year of psycho-therapy, and finally the two of us sadly agreed that things just weren't working out.

After we'd split, our lives suddenly took far different turns, as if we'd been spring-loaded to take off in new directions. I began studying Buddhist meditation; went on retreats in Nepal, Thailand, and here in the States; and found myself at the feet of dozens of spiritual sages who invariably spoke of the impermanence of everything. I knew about impermanence, having ended a marriage that was supposed to last as long as we both would live. But somehow, hearing it spoken by teachers I considered wise gave me solace. I also put myself through Union Theological Seminary in New York City and earned a master's in divinity.

Meanwhile Wanda launched herself into physical pursuits, becoming a luminary in the local contra dance, zydeco, and swing-dance community—a scene the two of us had never set foot in when we'd been together. She occasionally invited me to dances at a local parish hall or rec center near our homes in upstate New York. Sometimes, when I missed her, I'd show up. I'd pick her out of the crowd and wave, and she'd scoot over and guide me onto the floor, where I'd hobble along under her patient instruction as some of her suitors looked on. I can keep in step to rock-and-roll, but to this music, I was like a rusty engine that's reluctant to turn over. Wanda and I would laugh at how clumsy I was. Then I'd watch her dance with another man, the two of them seeming to glide across the floor.

The remorse I'd felt about initiating the divorce diminished when I saw Wanda enjoying life on her own. From time to time, we'd talk on the phone and trade stories about our latest romantic escapades. It turned out she and I were better friends than we'd been spouses: happier, more candid with each other, and less prone to bickering.

I had not seen Wanda for several months when she phoned me in April

2001 to tell me she was having surgery to remove a large mass in her abdomen. As I penciled in the date on my calendar, she told me not to worry, said it was nothing. And off she went with her latest beau to a Cajun-music festival in New Orleans.

I have always liked Wanda's family, and they have always liked me. Even after the divorce, I was invited to holiday dinners, birthday picnics, and Christmas services at their church. Wanda was Chinese American; her father had emigrated from Beijing and her mother from Shanghai in the 1940s, both fleeing the communist takeover. They'd met in New York City, married, and moved to suburban New Jersey, where I met Wanda while working at a newspaper. I was a young reporter, and she was an intern in the paper's graphic-design department. A middle-class, Connecticut-raised WASP, I was charmed by Wanda's Asian beauty. Although she and her two siblings were as American as I was, her parents were still very Chinese, and their culture seemed exotic to me. Her mother spoke with an accent I found hard to understand. Her father showed me sawtooth-edged, black-and-white photos of the house where he'd grown up, a palatial estate in Beijing that had been confiscated by the communist regime and turned into a barracks for the People's Liberation Army. Wanda and her family seemed less tormented by the guilt, worry, and conflict that droned on in my family and friends, and this held a certain allure for me.

On the day of Wanda's operation, I joined her mother, father, older sister Frieda, and brother-in-law Peter at the hospital. Wanda maintained her silly, often droll sense of humor throughout the pre-op. As the nurses rolled her on the gurney into the operating room, she held up the hand not tethered to the IV and cranked it side to side, like Queen Elizabeth waving from her Rolls-Royce. Several hours later, we met with her surgeon. We learned that a softball-sized pelvic mass had been removed in a total hysterectomy. He appeared disconcerted; the tissue, he said, would be sent to a lab for a biopsy, and the results would take a couple of days. Wanda would remain in the hospital to recover.

One evening, a few days later, I walked into her room after a stressful day at the office. Wanda was on the phone, snapping at the hospital switch-board operator—unusual behavior for her; Wanda was usually courteous to a fault. And she was glaring at the foot of her bed. The way I figured it, she had just been sliced open and was in pain. Of course she was irritable. Seeing me, she hung up and started to cry.

"I don't have good news," she said.

Whatever had bothered me at work that day fell away, and I rushed to her bedside and cupped one of her hands in mine. I imagined some infection, or perhaps she would need another operation.

"What is it?" I asked, caressing her long, black hair.

"It's cancer," she said.

Ovarian. And it was serious.

I laid my head on Wanda's lap and sobbed.

In the years we'd been apart, Wanda and I had each had several lovers who'd come and gone, but neither of us had remarried, nor were we seeing anyone at that time. This gave us the freedom to be with each other without competing love interests at the margins. I spent hours with Wanda in the cramped living room of her apartment, which adjoined her parents' house, an hour's drive from mine in New York State, where they had moved a few years before. A hospital bed her maternal grandmother had used in her final years was set up there. I also accompanied Wanda and her sister on trips to Boston's Dana-Farber/Brigham and Women's Cancer Center, where Wanda was treated with punishing, nauseating rounds of chemotherapy that kept her down for days. It was an aggressive regimen. She had a rare and virulent form of cancer—clear-cell—and it was at stage IV, which meant that the cancer had gotten into the liver. Stage IV can be treated but is terminal; few live beyond five years. In the aftermath of these treatments, Wanda would sometimes call me to gripe about the pain or for comfort, often weeping.

I tried to appear strong in the face of Wanda's weakening condition and, to some extent, my own. I visited her, ran errands for her, and sometimes cooked for her while the earth tilted us into summer and then fall. The September 11 attacks left Wanda and her sister stranded in Oregon, where they had spent a week learning *qigong* from a renowned Chinese master, hoping this ancient healing practice might help Wanda get well again. A few days later, when Peter and I drove to the Newark airport to pick them up, we could see, across the New Jersey tidal marshes, clouds of smoke from the still-smoldering remains of the Twin Towers. With all the death and dying in the air, I was elated to see Wanda alive at the gate. We hugged, and for a moment, I had the idea that everything was going to be fine.

For most of October, Wanda's condition remained relatively stable; her oncologist seemed encouraged by her response to the experimental brew of chemotherapy he'd prescribed and perhaps to the qigong. Then one November morning, Frieda called me.

"Something bad is happening with Wanda," she said, her voice distant from the poor cell phone connection. Peter had gone into the apartment to get Wanda, she said, and found her lying upstairs on a stripped bed in a spare bedroom, disoriented and barely cognizant. An ambulance was on the way.

"Jim's here!" exclaimed Frieda, when I parted the baby blue privacy curtain at the emergency room. Wanda, stretched out on a gurney, looked at me. There was no spark of recognition. Her head stayed tilted to the left, and her eyes were wide, as if she were shocked by the condition in which she found herself. The sole movement in that tight space was Wanda's left arm, which slowly rose and fell like a machine, as if to push back from her face the thick, black hair she'd once had. Doctors say hearing is the last of the senses to go, and I wondered if Wanda was listening as her family and I discussed her condition. I passed my hand lightly over her head to let her know I was there.

Wanda was admitted for observation and a battery of tests to determine what, exactly, had gone wrong with her brain. I spent my days and nights at the hospital, while a handful of office colleagues took on a good portion of my work. I had barely noticed the changing of the seasons that year, and when I did finally notice, it was through the sealed, grimy window of Wanda's fourth-floor room. The tops of the trees had gone bare, and the people on the broken sidewalks had thick clothes on, their shoulders hunched against the cold and puffs of steam coming from their mouths. I wanted so much to be out in the world; I wanted Wanda to be out there too—on the street, making plans, living life.

Wanda had a room to herself, and the night nurses let me stay past visiting hours. With the very real possibility of death hovering near, the world outside the window became increasingly irrelevant. The lines between day and night, the known and the unknowable, were beginning to blur. Even the fact of our divorce seemed to get erased.

I tried to get some rest in two tangerine-colored chairs I'd pushed together, but I never could sleep sitting up. To distract myself, I slipped on the headphones of the portable cassette player we'd brought for Wanda. (We'd thought music might comfort her.) I pushed the Play button. Van Morrison's "Carrying a Torch" came on.

Wanda had made the tape, labeled "Mellow Music," several weeks earlier. She'd put the Van Morrison song on it, she'd told me, because it reminded her of us. Sometimes we'd joked that when we got old and feeble, we'd shack up together in a nursing home. Now, delirious from insomnia, I gazed at Wanda's wasted form in the pale gray light and listened to Van Morrison beseech his lost lover to "reconnect and move further into the light." It was as if everything under me—the earth itself—had been pulled away, and I was plunging through a dark space, nowhere to go but down. I felt that by not wanting children and initiating the breakup of our marriage, I'd committed a heinous crime, and now I was being punished. Selfish bastard that I was, I'd stayed involved with Wanda even after we'd split up, perhaps thwarting her chances to get remarried and have the child she wanted. I'd read that not having children can increase a woman's risk of ovarian cancer—so that, too, was my fault.

Early the next morning, I was awakened by the sound of Wanda gurgling on vomit. After being admitted, she'd been given a morphine patch to ease her pain. I'd voiced a mild objection, having been told that, because she was "narcotic naive"—Wanda hardly even took aspirin— morphine could make her nauseous. Now I ran down the waxed hallway to tell the nurse that "my wife" was throwing up. It was the first time I had called Wanda my wife since we'd separated. I wanted the nurse to take my plea for help seriously, and somehow I thought that using the word *wife* would do the trick. But there was another, less calculated, reason: as I had vowed nearly twenty years before, I still cherished Wanda as if she were my wife, in sickness and in health.

The nurse came and wiped green bile from Wanda's chin, and despite my misgivings, I agreed Wanda should keep the morphine patch on. A few minutes later, though, just as I thought Wanda had drifted back to sleep, she started heaving again. I called the nurse back, and this time I took it upon myself to peel the morphine patch off Wanda's pale, blue-veined chest.

"She doesn't want morphine," I snarled, as if it were the nurse's fault it had been put there in the first place.

I'd been awake barely a half-hour, and already the day had taken its toll on me. Left alone in the room, I climbed into bed with Wanda. I thought that if she couldn't see or hear me, perhaps she could feel me. The rubber-coated mattress crinkled under my weight. Her emaciated form lay still as I curled against her, fetal-like, and nuzzled her neck. Wanda fell back to sleep, and after a few moments, so did I. It was the first time we'd been in the same bed together in eight years, and in a strange way, it felt like home. When her family doctor showed up later that morning, I was startled awake and felt intruded upon, as if he'd barged into our bedroom.

A couple of days later, tests revealed that the cancer cells had wormed their way into Wanda's skull, causing the brain tissue to swell. The neurologist described the condition as "impossible to treat."

So that was that. Her words were like a door gently closing, the lock quietly clicking into place. Wanda's family and I were drained of all the hope that had buoyed us through the previous six months—and there'd been plenty, I realized the moment it was snatched away. Wanda was brought home in an ambulance and put back in her grandmother's hospital bed to die.

I don't know when the idea first occurred to me, but I began to consider asking Wanda's family if we could hold a remarriage ceremony. I could not give Wanda back her life or undo the divorce. I couldn't even offer my help: the errands had all been done; the trips to Boston were over. Love was all I had left to give, and the ceremony would be a declaration of that. It would not be a legal marriage; Wanda was incapable of consenting. But I believed she would have wanted it. There had remained a sort of low blue flame of love between us, the kind Van Morrison sings about in the song on Wanda's tape. Wanda and I—and also her family and I—still carried that torch for each other.

At first, I was reluctant to make my request, for fear her family might be upset. But the idea of us carrying to our graves the broken promise I had made to Wanda in our first marriage ceremony—to be together "till death do us part"—troubled me. When I timidly mentioned the idea to her family, they were thrilled; they'd been thinking the same thing but couldn't bring themselves to ask me.

The family's minister came to the apartment to perform the ceremony. I spoke of the love that had kept Wanda and me and her family connected through the years. The minister read from the Song of Solomon ("Love is strong as death") and Ecclesiastes ("For everything there is a season"). Then he read some vows for me to respond to with "I will" and "I do." I wondered whether Wanda heard any of it. Could she see the small circle of friends and family members who had gathered round us? When it was over, Wanda's mother opened her arms to me, and we held one another tight, both of us weeping. Wanda's younger brother, whom I hardly knew, suddenly embraced me and said, "Welcome back."

During the night, I kept vigil, sleeping fitfully and dreamlessly in a twin bed perpendicular to Wanda's. Her breathing had grown labored and painful to listen to—somewhere between a snore and a wheeze. Each night her condition deteriorated, and she often gasped as if being strangled, which maybe she was, as death tightened its grip.

In the predawn hours of December 6, five days after we'd brought her home from the hospital, Wanda's labored breathing awakened me, louder than ever. Spit that looked like strained peas pooled in the corners of her mouth and on the collar of the thin cotton hospital gown. Normally squeamish about bodily excretions, I tended to Wanda's without a second thought. Her mother and I had already changed Wanda's soiled undergarments several times, both of us noticing how her right foot was turning ever deeper shades of purple from lack of circulation. I had little reaction to all of this. Perhaps I had closed down, or perhaps I was opening up. Buddhists speak of how, if you can train the mind not to get attached to human suffering, you can benevolently enter any "hell realm" of existence like a swan with wings spread, swooping down on a lake. I now got up and wiped Wanda's chin with a handful of tissue, then passed my hand over her head, trying to comfort her. Her eyes were wide and fixed on something beyond me, beyond all of us.

I climbed back into my bed and fell asleep. When I woke again, a cold, gray December dawn was showing through the tops of the skeletal trees outside the windows. This time it was not Wanda's breathing that had awakened me; it was the silence.

A couple of hours later, a gray panel van arrived from the funeral home, and two men lumbered out to retrieve Wanda's body. If I'd had any sense, I would have backed off and let the men do their job, but I was not yet ready to abdicate my responsibilities to Wanda. I helped lift her body off the hospital bed and onto a gurney, bedsheets and all. I'd prepared to lift a heavy weight, but Wanda's frame was so insubstantial, so eaten up by cancer, I could have picked her up by myself. One of the men had put a pale blue corduroy body bag on the gurney, and I zipped it up over Wanda the way you would a child's parka on a winter day. Wanda disappeared, and I realized that this would be the last time I'd ever see her.

As I helped wheel the gurney out to the van, I suddenly insisted that the body be moved headfirst, and the driver obliged. Years ago, I'd read about an ancient Hindu tradition: you carry a body feetfirst at the start of its trip to the funeral pyre, so the spirit can remember its earthly life; for the second half of the journey, you turn the body headfirst, to help facilitate the spirit's departure from its material existence. After the van had pulled away, I turned to Susan, a friend of Wanda's and mine whom I'd called that morning, and I collapsed into her arms and fell apart.

A part of me died with Wanda, a part I was glad to see go: my resistance to love. I'd often put distance between myself and others as a way to keep from feeling trapped or getting hurt. I'd delivered wearying criticisms of people I thought were less than perfect, as if I were any better than them. Living like that had been a long, hard battle with many casualties, the most wounded sometimes being me. I think that during all those silent-meditation sessions; in all the time I'd spent listening to the wisdom of renowned teachers, theologians, and sages; in all the millions of words I'd read in profound spiritual tracts, I'd been trying to learn how to love. But no amount of meditation or yoga or studies of scriptures could have given me that. Wanda's death put me in touch with one of the highest orders of human existence: to love others as though we are all dying all the time, because the plain truth of the matter is that we are. For a long time I didn't know how to articulate this new feeling, even to myself. Then a couple of years ago I heard k.d. lang sing a Leonard Cohen song in which love is described as "a cold and broken hallelujah." And I thought, *Yes, that's it*. In this love, I found rest from a sort of homesickness that had afflicted me all my life.

It was not long before my days reassembled themselves into a more or less familiar shape, which was a sort of relief. But I began to forget how, in my hour of grief, I'd cherished my existence and the people around me. Years later, it sometimes feels as if I have to reach across a great psychic distance to get in touch with the way I felt then, as though it lay beyond the curve of the earth.

I have not remarried. From time to time I wonder if I will ever again feel for anyone else what I felt for Wanda in our final months together. And if not, then what? Sometimes someone will ask me if I regret not having children. No, I say. And yes. I don't know whether being a father would have sustained the love I felt as Wanda died. Parents I know have told me that this is what having children does to you: it opens your heart. One mother said that what you feel bringing a person into the world is akin to what you feel seeing someone out of it. Perhaps I didn't have children with Wanda because I was afraid of feeling too much; I don't know. What I do know is that I miss Wanda's features—her brown eyes, round face, delicate frame, and silly sense of humor—some of which appear in the children of her siblings, some of which would no doubt have been replicated in our children. And maybe if Wanda and I had brought a child or two into the world, it wouldn't be such a struggle for me now to recollect the love I felt when she was dying.

So my pen hovers over the little boxes on those forms. My own internal compass tells me I'm widowed. Even if we'd never had that remarriage ceremony, I still would have felt married to Wanda when she died. Our divorce did not end our relationship, and for me, her death made it even more lasting and unfathomable.

For a while after she died, I checked "widowed," hoping the clerks would notice it and tease a story out of me. It was like a little flag I waved. I wanted sympathy, to be seen as more than just another client, customer, patient, student. I was also hoping to trigger a discussion of a similar loss on their part so we could commiserate, like strangers in a snowstorm, and I could give voice to the huge, uncertain emotions swirling inside me.

Legally, however, I am not widowed. So, reluctantly, I check the "divorced" box. But what is a marriage if not the depth of feeling you have for each other? It's only the love between two people that's real, that lasts. Everything else just comes and goes.

PART FIVE

Growing Apart

Making Friends with Heartbreak

SUSAN PIVER

After a breakup, what helps more than anything is to be gentle toward yourself. Meditation instructor Susan Piver knows this firsthand; she's been there.

A FEW MONTHS AFTER my longtime boyfriend and I had broken up, I was charged with conducting a business meeting at a restaurant over lunch. I was pretty sure I was on the road to recovery from the breakup and had been genuinely looking forward to this opportunity to discuss an exciting new project with the other attendees, colleagues I respected and admired. I made a reservation at a favorite restaurant, which we had been to many times before and was always delicious. *Yes,* I thought, *I'm going to be okay. I have a good job. I work with wonderful folks. Our meeting is going to be fun. I am moving on, damn it.*

So I drove to the meeting with a lovely feeling of things returning to normal. The seven of us, as I had requested, were seated at the only round table in the restaurant large enough to accommodate a group of that size. We were settling ourselves around the table, waving hello, pulling out papers, and turning off pagers, when everything completely fell apart for me. *The waiter had brought us a basket of jalapeño cheddar-cheese cornbread.*

Oh no. He loved jalapeño cheddar-cheese cornbread. A mere glimpse of those crumbly, orangey squares flecked with green blotted out all feelings of normality and, once again, my world turned upside down. Tears stung the back of my eyeballs, and I gruffly pushed back my chair to try to make it to the ladies' room, but not quite in time—the tears had already begun to fall. *There's no hope,* I thought. Just when I thought I was getting my life back, a piece of bread caused it to disintegrate once again.

I sat down in one of the stalls and tried to cry without making any noise, which, as anyone who has attempted this knows, only leads to a bulbous nose and a Mount Rushmore–sized headache. Somehow I soldiered on and made it through the meeting, and when I got home at the end of the day, I was too tired to cry anymore, so I just lay on the couch. For about six hours. When I finally dragged myself to bed, I thought, *I'll never get over this. Why? Why do the waves of grief just keep coming? What is happening here, and will it ever end?*

At this point, I realized that there was very little, maybe nothing, I could do to predict, modulate, and manage these unpredictable waves of grief. Trying to fight them would be like trying not to have nightmares by staying awake all night just in case one might arise. It was just too exhausting. I had to accept that these episodes were simply a part of my life for the time being, and I was going to have to learn to deal with them instead. But how?

Soon after this, I was attending a talk by a Tibetan Buddhist monk at a local meditation center. He was young, not yet thirty, but already highly respected as a scholar and spiritual adept. After talking about overcoming obstacles such as depression and anxiety, he was asked about how we can manage our emotions in a world of ever-increasing danger and uncertainty, how to cope with feelings of paralyzing dread about our safety and the future of the planet. The monk said, "When you are filled with fear, anxiety, or other difficult emotions, the first thing you should always do is make friends with them." Rather than fighting off unpleasant feelings, it is always best to soften, open, and invite them in. Fighting wastes valuable time. Allowing them acknowledges the reality of that particular moment and makes it easier to address your circumstances intelligently. For example, if you're walking down a dark street trying to pretend you're not afraid, you might miss the valuable signals fear offers you when you tune in and open to it.

And so it is with a broken heart, or any other problem, really. You may have been taught to attack a problem when you encounter it, either by trying to fix it right away or else eradicating it. I'm not suggesting that this is never a good idea, but there is another option that is not often thought of, which is to extend the hand of friendship to your situation. This is an extraordinary thing to do. Making friends with your broken heart, instead of trying to mend it or banish it, begins by simply making room for it to exist. You could even invite it to sit down with you, since you've probably been hating it or trying to ignore it. When grief and disappointment threaten to overwhelm you, instead of bemoaning them, turning away, or shrinking in fear of them, you could feel them. Instead of trying to shout them down, either by talking yourself out of what you're feeling ("It's all his fault, anyway"), making up a story about what it all means ("I always attract the wrong guys"), or collapsing on the couch with a bottle of gin (to deaden the pain), invite your feelings in and get to know them.

For example, when you feel grief, where does it manifest in your body? Does it weigh down your chest, close your throat, or make your shoulders ache? How about disappointment or anger or any of the other feelings that have become your companions? If your emotion had a color, what would it be? If your emotion could speak to you (instead of the other way around), what would it say? When you suddenly feel a pang of emotion, whether positive or negative, can you go back and pinpoint the exact moment it arose? These are useful questions. Just like getting to know a new friend, the first step is simply to find out about her.

This process is really, really hard, so you need to appreciate yourself and what you are going through. So many problems result from the inability to simply be kind to yourself. Please develop some sympathy for yourself, which is different from self-pity or self-indulgence. Imagine if you knew that your best friend or your child or your mom was going through what you are experiencing—wouldn't your heart ache for her? Wouldn't you feel that if only there was something you could do to help, you would do it? Wouldn't you think about her night and day with kindness, hoping for her to find peace?

Ask yourself honestly: have you felt these things about yourself?

If you have, that is wonderful; you are a great friend. If you haven't, you could try to offer kindness to yourself. You know that the ultimate kindness, the best thing you can do for a friend, is simply to be there with her and for her when she's falling apart. Offering advice is not helpful unless you've been asked directly to give it. You know that trying to talk her out of what she's feeling or convince her that it's not a big deal is unkind. Telling her to buck up already is certainly not helpful. What helps more than anything? Simple, unquestioning, ultrapatient companionship. Be by her side. Take her to a movie to get her mind off the situation. Check in with her throughout the day just so she'll know someone is thinking of her. Listen to her patiently, no matter how many times you've heard the story; feel sad with her when she cries and relieved when her spirits begin to rise.

What helps more than anything is to be gentle toward yourself. Gentleness doesn't mean being all "poor baby" or coddling yourself in any way. Real gentleness has way more precision and intelligence than that. Gentleness means simply that you acknowledge and embrace your own experience from moment to moment, without judgment. Without trying to fix it. Without feeling ashamed of it or, if you do feel ashamed of it, you do not feel ashamed of your shame! In this way, gentleness is actually an advanced form of bravery. You aren't afraid to take on your own suffering, even though you don't know how or when it will end; still, you agree to feel it. Somehow, this acceptance begins to calm things down. In this way, on its own timetable, gentleness begins to pacify even the most raging emotions. Gentleness is the spiritual, emotional warrior's most powerful weapon.

The best way to cultivate gentleness toward yourself, thought by thought and moment by moment, is through the sitting practice of meditation. In fact, meditation, which is sitting with your self, your thoughts, emotions, and yearnings, and simply allowing them to be as they are, is the practice of gentleness itself. There is no better teacher than this.

Most likely, there will be only a few times in your life when you'll reach the limit of what you can bear. It may be from falling ill, the death of a parent, or even the loss of a most precious possession, such as your home, and of course, it can also be because of a broken heart. To face these extraordinary times, you need to take extraordinary measures. Most of the tactics touted as "extraordinary measures," however, are really ways of escaping the reality of what we must face, our emotions. Certainly drinking, drugging, random sex, and sleeping all the time are ways to avoid emotional pain, but even healthier means, such as positive thought, physical exercise, therapy, or simply forcing yourself to move on are also methods of stepping away from what ails you rather than toward it. Stepping toward it and going into it do not just mean lying around crying all the time. It means meeting your emotions and relating to them, not as enemies to be conquered, but as wounded friends from the front who need your loving attention. As Zen teacher and poet John Tarrant says, "Attention is the most basic form of love. Through it, we bless and are blessed."

Of Course I'm Angry

GABRIEL COHEN

As his marriage falls apart, Gabriel Cohen obsesses over all the things his wife has done to make him angry. But a chance encounter shows him the anger is his alone and serves no good purpose.

THREE YEARS AGO I was standing in a real estate office, filling out a rental application, when out of the corner of my eye, I saw a big man enter and approach the realtor. The stranger muttered something, then shoved the young man. I thought he was just kidding—a friend roughhousing?—until he pinned the realtor against a wall and started punching holes in the Sheetrock, four of them, circling the frightened man's head.

Breathless, I ran out to the store next door and urged the woman behind the counter to call the police. "The guy next door is about to be killed!"

I tiptoed back to check on the realtor. Thankfully, his assailant had disappeared, leaving him alive and unhurt, but the man was still trembling.

"Who was that?" I asked. "Some crazy person off the street?"

"No," the realtor replied. "His ex-wife used to work here. He was drunk, and he was looking for her."

I walked out of the office into a New York heat wave, a day so hot that the asphalt was threatening to melt. I was in the middle of the worst period of my life: a month before, my own wife had suddenly—without warning or apology—walked out of our marriage.

I thought about that stranger's anger, and I thought about my own.

I considered myself a generally cheerful person, prone to corny jokes and bad impressions of TV characters, but that jovial self-image had been severely tested during the last few months of my marriage. Our landlord had decided to sell the house my wife and I were renting an apartment in. Though she and I had gotten along well for four years, our search for a new home led to all sorts of disagreements, and then to outright verbal fights (which pointed to other hidden problems in our relationship).

After our marriage fell apart, I trudged through the city streets, praying that I could find an affordable place on my own. I spent endless hours playing a mental loop in which I railed against my ex-wife, her friends, and even her therapist. At around that time, I stumbled across a poster for a Buddhist talk. I knew little about Buddhism; I saw it as a foreign, esoteric religion full of rituals and chanting, or a New Age fad for rock stars and Hollywood actors. But the title of the talk grabbed my attention: How to Deal with Anger (not—as my preconceptions might have led me to expect—How to Bliss Out and Pretend You're Not Really Angry). Under ordinary circumstances, I would have passed on by, but I was suffering and desperate. What did I have to lose?

That very first talk turned my whole world upside down—or right side up. I was greatly surprised to hear that if I was angry at my wife, my wife was not the problem. My problem was *my anger.*

I used to think of the spiritual path as a detached, solo journey, like Moses trekking up the mountain or the Buddha wandering off to sit under his bodhi tree. I imagined how challenging it would be to renounce life's pleasures and meditate in a cave. Now I realize that life offers a much more common but just as powerful spiritual trial: just try getting along with one other person for the rest of your life. Tie the knot. In good times, the rewards are great: the intimacy, the support, the joy of being loved and of loving someone else. Sometimes, though, the positive energy of a marriage seems to derail, to twist, to spiral into a negative whirlwind. It almost appears as if the more good energy you put into a relationship, the more bad feeling can come howling out the other side.

In my case, I was sorely tempted to blame my wife for our problems. After all, I had gone into marriage with the understanding that it would inevitably entail struggling through some hard times; she was the one who had refused to put in the hard work that any relationship requires. I thought she was *making me* feel angry—and heartbroken and betrayed and all that other fun stuff. I mean, I knew my anger was an internal feeling, but it felt as if it was coming to me from her, as if it could leap from one person to the other. I didn't see my anger as a sign of my own irrationality; I thought it made perfect sense. My wife had behaved unreasonably—*of course* I was getting upset.

As I mentioned, though, that talk on anger rocked my view.

It took place in a yoga studio. The teacher held up a book. "How many of you think this exists independently of your mind?"

Everyone in the audience raised their hand.

As the teacher led us to see, though, our only way of knowing the book was there was by filtering our perception of it through our own minds. And that's true of every single thing in our lives: the objects around us, the people, our concepts, *everything*. Our entire experience of life is shaped by how we perceive and how we think.

Normally, we believe that we need to reshape our external circumstances to improve how we feel (more money, a better job, a more accommodating spouse), but that's a huge, never-ending, continually frustrating quest. The more feasible, achievable goal is to transform our lives by changing how we think about them. As the eighth-century sage Shantideva put it, if we want to avoid stepping on thorns, we can't possibly cover the whole world with leather—but we *can* cover our own feet.

Somehow, I realized early on that being pissed off at my ex was not making me feel better. I needed to find a more positive way out of my suffering. The fact that my emotions only existed inside my own head was great news; it meant that they were not dependent on my ex-wife, or how the legal proceedings developed, or on any other external factors. I could improve my experience of divorce by taking responsibility for my feelings and by learning how to train my mind. And so I set out on a journey of internal exploration, observing my thoughts like a scientist peering at electrons buzzing around inside a cloud chamber. I made some fundamental discoveries.

I found that I was not "an angry person"—I was simply a person experiencing angry *thoughts*. Like all thoughts, they were just temporary, just passing through my head like storms through a clear blue sky. They didn't have the power to damage the inherent clarity of my mind. And they couldn't force me to act in an angry way. I learned that it was possible to put a little pause, a breathing space, between an external event and my reaction to it in order to discover a broader range of options.

As I probed deeper, I realized that—in almost every case—my anger arose out of a deep, internal sense of *hurt*. That feeling was uncomfortable, often intolerable, and I would try to get rid of it by projecting it outward. That seemed to offer some sense of relief, but it had pained my wife and damaged our relationship.

Often, my hurt arose out of a perceived sense of injustice. Like legions of foolish men before me, I believed that being right was the essential thing. When conflicts arose, I argued like an expensive trial lawyer. I won some battles, but I lost the war.

I don't want to overstate how angry I was. My wife and I actually got along very peacefully and lovingly for the great majority of our time together. I'm generally pretty upbeat and laid-back, and I have friends who say that they can hardly even *imagine* me angry.

On the other hand, that Buddhist talk made me realize that I was probably underestimating how angry I—and most people—really are much of the time. We tend to believe that anger is an aberration, an emotion that only arises in exceptional circumstances. But pick up any newspaper and you'll see how prevalent it is in the world at large: abuse, assault, murder, war. And it's pervasive in our daily lives. We're peeved that it starts raining just as we decide to go out for a walk. We're disappointed that we didn't win the lottery (even if we didn't buy a ticket!). We're irate because our parents didn't love us enough or loved us too much. We're aggrieved that our life is not turning out as we wish or believe it should. Some of us can't acknowledge our anger; we suppress it and become depressed, or we try to salve it with alcohol or food or shopping—or we run away. (If you doubt that there's an unacknowledged current of anger underlying your daily existence, just notice how it flares up the instant someone cuts you off in traffic or steals your parking space. Did it arise out of nowhere, or was it already there?)

Among all our spurs to anger, why is a failed marriage so especially powerful? Partly, it's because our expectations are so high and unrealistic. We buy into a fairy tale that our spouse will relieve us of all our existential suffering and loneliness; we believe that they should make us happy all the time. That's not love; it's an ego-based delusion called *desirous attachment*. When that false ideal falls apart, it's quickly replaced by disappointment and hostility. It's much easier to blame our spouse than to acknowledge the fundamental wrongness of our own view.

It's not a thin line between love and hate; Buddhism says that true love is *never* the cause of suffering. It's a thin line between unreasonable expectations and the stinging disenchantment that arises when they can't be met. A big part of the solution is learning to let go of our expectations of what *should* happen and to be more accepting of what life actually brings. As the thirteenth-century Zen teacher and philosopher Dogen beautifully put it, "A flower falls, even though we love it; and a weed grows, even though we do not love it."

As I developed a meditation practice, I came to understand that my feelings of disappointment and hurt and injustice were all rooted in the same toxic soil: an inflated sense of the primacy of my own needs and desires—what Buddhists call *self-cherishing*. My anger was a childish wail of complaint: "What about *me*?"

A remarkable meditation helped me start letting go of my self-centeredness and resentment. I became familiar with the technique of imagining that I was exhaling my tensions and frustrations as dark smoke and that I was inhaling a clear, blissful light. One day, though, after another talk on anger, the teacher offered an astonishing, counterintuitive exercise. She said that if we were angry with someone, we should imagine breathing in *their* suffering as dark smoke and that we should imagine breathing toward *them* a clear, blissful light. In the early days of my divorce, the last thing I wanted was to imagine that I was taking on my wife's troubles, but when I tried the meditation, it had a profound effect: it helped me to see her as a suffering person in her own right. I had already found that when my heart was full of anger, it held no room for compassion. While doing this meditation, I discovered that the reverse was also true.

Buddhists say that the antidote to anger is patience. One thing that has helped me move toward that goal has been learning to see that things do not inherently exist in the way that I perceive them to (the Buddhist concept of emptiness). That may sound abstract and intellectual, but it's easy to apply to relationships. When Zen master Shunryu Suzuki was asked to sum up the essence of his philosophy, he replied with just three words: "Not necessarily so." If I get riled up now, I repeat those words to myself, a reminder that my perception of what's going on is undoubtedly incomplete and likely faulty. The anger I perceive in someone else may be arising out of hurt; their seeming stubbornness may cover insecurity and fear.

Did all this new knowledge miraculously enable me to eradicate my anger? Of course not. But at least I started getting better at recognizing it when it first arose and calming myself before I might act on it.

Eventually, I came to see that anger was a false friend. Though it might seem to bolster me, to save me from depression, to keep me moving forward, it worked against me. Each impetuous e-mail, each vengeful riposte, each passive-aggressive refusal to respond—they all came back to bite me in the end. Acting out of anger is *never* the skillful thing to do.

You might think of certain exceptions. What about anger directed against social injustice? And isn't it necessary and therapeutic to express some anger?

I can think of at least three answers to these objections.

First, anger causes us to perceive its object in a distorted way. We turn the person we're mad at into an ogre. We become unable to see their good qualities, and we get pumped full of a blinding adrenaline that often causes our interactions to spiral out of control. Anger leads us to see things in a polarized, sharply dualistic way. We believe we're good; we believe our enemies are evil.

If you think that's a helpful way to look at conflict, just look at what it has done for the Israelis and Palestinians, Hutus and Tutsis, Armenians and Turks. Of course, it's important to work against injustice, but we need to do so wisely, with clear eyes and a compassionate, understanding view of all sides. As Gandhi, Martin Luther King Jr., and the Dalai Lama have so ably demonstrated, a calm mind gets better results. These wise leaders were able to see that, just as our anger is a delusion arising out of our suffering, the anger of our "enemies" is also a delusion, like a sickness in their minds. We should fight the delusion, not the people who suffer from it.

Second, though some therapists tout the benefits of expressing anger in a controlled way, such as punching a pillow, recent research in neuroscience contradicts that notion: if you punch a pillow, you're actually exercising and reinforcing your brain's neural pathways for aggression.

Finally, our anger damages us as well as the object of our wrath. It increases our heart rate, elevates our blood pressure, and has other serious health effects. As the saying goes, anger is an acid that corrodes the vessel that holds it. This seems stupidly obvious to me now, but when I was tromping around the streets of Brooklyn, running my resentful little mental loops, I failed to realize that they had absolutely no effect on my wife. I was just working myself into an increasingly agitated state—punching holes, in effect, in a wall that only I could see. I was carrying around an entirely unhelpful burden, and I had to resolve to set it down.

In case I needed a more forceful demonstration of the dangers of anger, life soon provided one. A few minutes after I left that real estate office, I came across another realtor. Miraculously, she drove me straight to a fantastic apartment, in a big old Victorian house with a front porch and a back patio, a stained glass window, and even a chandelier. By New York standards, the rent was cheap. It wasn't until a few weeks later—just before I moved in—that I found out why. It turned out that my landlord had been having troubles with his own marriage.

One night, in a fit of rage, he had killed his wife.

In my new apartment.

The message could not have been clearer: this is what can happen if you let anger win.

Three years of working with Buddhist insights and practice have certainly not turned me into a saint, but occasionally I see evidence of progress.

My writing desk faces a window that looks out on the street. My neighborhood is generally quiet, but several days ago a stranger parked a luxury car directly outside. After a few minutes, its car alarm started going off—the worst kind, the one where the horn continually bleats. I sat there trying to work, getting increasingly frustrated and annoyed. Finally, I wrote a note, and then I marched out and stuck it under the windshield wiper. (What kind of note? Let's put it this way, the salutation read, "Dear Asshole.")

When I came back inside, I sat there listening to the alarm. And I stared at my note. It took a while, but eventually my new training kicked in. At first, I thought my blast of anger would cause the owner of the car to feel regretful and ashamed; I finally realized that it would only make him angry in return.

I replaced it with a new note. I did my best to keep my emotions out of it. Calmly, I explained that the car alarm was broken. What else did I have to say? I didn't need to inflate the problem by adding all sorts of self-righteousness and drama; I just called it to his attention, and then I let it go.

At the end of a long path, after extensive mental training, we might hope to become completely free of anger. In the meantime, it can act as a fire that consumes us or a bell that warns us when something is wrong—not with our circumstances, but with the way that we're thinking about them.

The choice is ours.

I Think We Should Stop Seeing Each Other

KAREN KISSEL WEGELA

Endings are painful, filled with uncertainty and groundlessness, but they also provide opportunity. Psychologist Karen Kissel Wegela shows how the notion of bardo—*the in-between state described in* The Tibetan Book of the Dead—*can help us to heal and move on.*

I WAS JUST EIGHTEEN and in my first year of college. I had been going out with Sam for about four months, and it was the first important relationship I'd been in. I was already fantasizing about our future life together.

One evening, he sat me down and said, "Karen, I think we should stop seeing each other." Everything seemed to stop. I felt shocked and uncertain. I could hardly formulate a response to what he had said.

For the first few seconds, nothing at all seemed to come. I felt disoriented; I don't think I felt much of my body. Then I felt a wave of heat come to my face. I began to shake. Then I felt a swirl of emotions: fear, sadness, anger, self-doubt, jealousy.

A stream of thoughts rushed through my mind: Was he going to go back to his former girlfriend? What was the matter with me? Had I done something wrong? What would I do now? How would I tell my friends? What about that great time we had two weeks ago? What a jerk he was anyway!

I was lost in thoughts about the past and future, doubts about myself, and judgments of him. I barely saw Sam sitting right in front of me. I mumbled something and dashed out of the room.

Like many of us, I believed that a good relationship was one that lasted forever. "Happily *ever* after." The truth is that all relationships change, and all of them end. Unless we die together, one of us leaves first. These days, even more commonly, one or the other of us will decide that the relationship has reached an ending. This is true of all kinds of relationships— those between friends, spouses, business colleagues, and teachers and students.

I once did a weeklong program of meditation and study held during spring break for the third-year students in the contemplative psychotherapy program at the Naropa Institute. Since it was held just seven weeks before they graduated, the focus of this program was on endings, and we studied portions of *The Tibetan Book of the Dead.*

In the evenings, we had talks and discussions about the text and engaged in some experiential exercises based on our study. The textures and patterns of endings became vivid and poignant. Sometimes people found themselves crying, feeling as though they might never stop. Other times people were furiously angry. Some people felt numb; some felt anxious. Some spent their time thinking about what they would do after graduation; still others refused to consider it at all. At the same time, all of these responses would fall apart again and again, and many would find themselves feeling shaky, uncertain, and tender.

A part of all relationships is facing their impermanence, their endings. In psychotherapy, we use the unbeautiful word *termination* to refer to the time preceding and the actual ending of therapeutic relationships. The notion of bardo presented in *The Tibetan Book of the Dead* is very helpful to students about to graduate, therapists working with clients on termination, and anyone for whom a relationship is ending or has ended.

Bardo refers to an in-between state. It is most often used in the Buddhist tradition to refer to the time between death and rebirth. The bardo experience is generally regarded as a time of great opportunity. There is a sense of heightened intensity as well as a feeling of great uncertainty and groundlessness. Because we cannot rely on our usual reference points and habitual patterns, the possibility that we might wake up and recognize the nature of mind is enhanced.

Regardless of whether one believes the accuracy of *The Tibetan Book of the Dead*'s description of the after-death experience, it provides a powerful metaphor of how we usually approach transitions. According to the text, in the Bardo of the Moment Before Death and in the Bardo of Dharmata, we are presented again and again with our own nature, yet we generally fail to recognize it because we tend to rely on our habitual styles of perception and projection. In the *Book of the Dead,* these projections appear as peaceful and wrathful deities. Rather than see that these are just the projections of our own nature, we see them as external beings who might help or harm us.

Finally, if we do not recognize our true nature, despite many chances to do so, we find ourselves wandering in the Bardo of Becoming, trying to either reenter our old body or find a new one. Driven by the momentum of karma—the speed of habitual mind—we find ourselves once again having to face birth, old age, sickness, and death.

How does all this relate to endings and transitions in our everyday lives? Often, the first time we let ourselves recognize that an ending is really coming, we feel the kind of disorientation I felt when Sam told me we should stop seeing each other. Our ordinary reference points fail us; we lose track of who and what we are; we don't know what we can count on.

This can actually be extremely helpful—if we are willing to tolerate it. It gives us a chance to see things just as they are. All of those reference points—"I'm Sam's girl," "I'm a student at Naropa," "I work as a therapist"—are impermanent. They hold no real solidity, and in moments when we feel the shock of impermanence, we glimpse the illusory quality of these relative reference points. As in the *Book of the Dead,* we might have a glimpse of our buddha nature, our basic goodness, our brilliant sanity—our unconditioned true nature.

However, we don't usually manage to stay that open. We are more likely, as I did, to fall into obsessive thinking or despair. We tend to speed up and lose track of where we are. We try to hang on, we try to reject the relationship first, or we try to avoid the whole thing.

Often we become caught in ambivalence; we want to do two conflicting things at the same time. We want to know the right thing to do, and we torture ourselves with our options: "Should I move to Oregon and look for a job, or should I stay put and see what happens?" "Should I call him up and try to talk, or should I wait and see what he does?" Or we drive ourselves nuts going over what happened, seeing if we can find an answer: "Is it his fault or my fault?" "Did I really understand what was taught, or did I fool everyone?"

This ambivalence is accompanied by a sense of building urgency and momentum. Sometimes it will build to a crescendo and then "pop," and we find ourselves once again on the spot in the present moment. This is another opportunity to wake up. Usually, however, we just start the whole thing up again.

The *Book of the Dead* offers a good suggestion for us. It tells us to "recognize and relax." In other words, we can try to come into the present moment and be with whatever is happening. We can hold both options and not have to choose until we have some clarity. We can befriend not-knowing. We can recognize that all of the fantasies we run are just the projections of our mind; they have no reality separate from us.

Furthermore, with respect to the Bardo of Becoming, we can recognize that we are trying to find a "new birth." One of the most difficult parts of working with transitions is the pressure we feel to replace the old "body" with a new one. We search for confirmation of ourselves by finding a new relationship, a new community, a new job. Obviously, there is no problem, in itself, with doing something new, but often we jump blindly into the next situation without taking the time to notice our experience of the ending of the last one.

Finally, the most important thing is to bring mindfulness and awareness to what is happening as the ending approaches and passes. Often we will try to apply old habitual patterns, but if we are curious about this, we might not get so caught up in them. We can notice the speed of mind that might arise. We can allow ourselves to feel all of the feelings that come—anxiety, self-doubt, relief, guilt, sadness, whatever it is. Ironically, if we let ourselves experience what is really happening, we might be surprised to discover openness and vulnerability that makes us more available to others.

When Relationships End

DAVID RICHO

Just as we can bring mindful awareness to the experience of being together, we can bring it to the process of breaking up, says psychotherapist David Richo. Here he offers guidance for the journey from grief to healing to a new beginning.

THERE SEEMS TO BE no better way to learn what a relationship is really about than to see how it ends and how we are in the ending. All relationships end—some with separation, some with divorce, some with death. This means that, in entering a relationship, we implicitly accept that the other will leave us or we will leave them. Grieving is therefore included in what we sign on for.

The grief at the end of a relationship comes from no longer getting our needs met. We think we only feel it at the very end, but we have probably felt it during the relationship too. At the end and afterward, we remember the grief we felt during the relationship, not only the grief we felt at the end. Perhaps we did not notice it before because we were raising children, having dinner, having sex, going to movies, sharing cocktails, hanging curtains. Ironically, the worse the relationship was, the worse our grief will be. This is because when we end a very difficult relationship, we are letting go not only of a partner but of all the hope and work we invested in trying to keep alive something that had expired long before. We thought wrongly— and sadly—that our partner's ability to meet our needs was in her somewhere, and all we had to do was keep trying to evoke that ability and someday we would see it emerge. Now we finally have to admit that such a someday will never come.

But we feel the pain most severely when we uselessly fight against a necessary ending, when we hold on at the point when we need to let go. What do we need to let go of? What we thought the relationship was and found out it was not, what we tried to make it into and could not, what we hoped it would become and saw that it did not, what we believed was there and was not there after all. The most painful element of grief may be this last realization that what we expected or longed for was not there to be had. How familiar and especially tormenting that may be if we had the same experience in childhood.

I grow up when I admit that neediness, loneliness, and longing persist in me in my adult life. There is always that child inside wanting more. He is the one who makes me buy those chocolate chip cookies when I stop at the store intending to buy only vegetables.

If we have stronger feelings after a relationship than we ever experienced while it was going on, it is a sign that our grief resembles and is reviving past losses. We are grieving more than just this ending. Many endings were stacked inside us, awaiting their chance for the attention of tears.

During a painful ending or in the midst of a crisis of infidelity or betrayal, our spiritual practice and all our psychological work may not restore us to serenity. Our obsessive thoughts prevent us from meditating for long, while psychological insights prove to be only palliatives. This does not reflect a deficiency in our program or practice, neither of which work best when adrenaline is flowing. If we cannot appreciate Mozart and the *Mona Lisa* at this time either, it does not mean art is useless. All bets are off when someone has hurt us. In such utter bereftness, the ego confronts its true face: frustrated, scared, caught in a painful attachment, powerless to alter what others may be doing to us.

The risky move is also the only reasonable option for us: to let go completely. This requires enormous discipline, because the ego wants to assert itself and regain its power. Our work during a breakup is also immensely simple: to witness rather than react or attempt to escape the pain. We let the chips fall where they may and use the pieces we are left with as the building blocks for whatever comes next.

Finally, leaving may not be about wanting to get out of the relationship completely. It may be a way of getting some space or breaking out of the doldrums rather than a conclusion on a partner's suitability. Many a relationship has ended when all that was needed was some time apart.

If you are wondering about whether to leave a relationship or not, it is crucial to discuss your concerns with your partner. Then it is wise for the two of you to see a competent therapist to address, process, and resolve your concerns together. As a start, it may be useful to ask yourself the following questions and notice if the majority of your answers are yes or no. Respond to these questions individually, and then you might compare your answers:

- Do you and your partner show one another love, respect, and support?

- Do you enjoy and feel safe in one another's company?

- Do you regularly make time for one another?

- Is this relationship fully in keeping with your own deepest needs, values, and wishes?

- Is your sex life together satisfactory?

- Are you remaining faithful to one another?

- Do you trust your partner?

- Are you and your partner willing to work on conflicts together?

- Are you keeping agreements with one another?

- Regarding past hurts, do you now live in an atmosphere of mended failures rather than of stubbornly held resentments?

- Does your partnership match what you always wanted for yourself in an intimate relationship?

- Are you together by choice rather than because of history, family, social convention, financial security, religious influence, the absence of an immediate alternative, or the inconvenience in or fear of separating?

- When you describe how you first met or how you first knew you were in love, is it with detail, enthusiasm, and a sense that it was fortunate?

- Does your inner trio—heart, head, gut—assent to continuing the relationship?

When a relationship ends by separation or divorce, there are some practical suggestions that may be helpful. First, we need a space in which to grieve alone and let go. To avoid this by jumping into a new relationship contradicts the course of nature. Grief work gives us an impetus for growth by helping us advance to a higher level of consciousness. The person I find immediately upon ending a relationship is likely to be at the same level of maturity as my ex-partner. The person I find when I have been alone for a while—and have had a chance to reflect, process, and grow from my experience—is more likely to be at a higher level of maturity.

As you grieve you are not available to others. Your children miss their absent parent, and thus they turn into mourners too. In turn, expect their grief to compound yours, because you are mirroring them. This is a normal element of grief within a family, especially since the family unit is lost.

The ending of a relationship does not have to be hateful and ego-competitive. A commitment to compassion can configure the process of ending as *hospicing,* not as slaying. Partners—or at least one of them—can let go of the relationship with loving-kindness.

Sleep disorders are to be expected at this time. You may also fall into your customary patterns of self-destruction—for example, overeating or undereating, addiction to a substance, or suicidal thoughts. Grief involves an ending, something our bodies may associate with a wish to die that has lain buried within us since childhood.

Therapy is crucial during this period; it can assist us in addressing, processing, and resolving issues as well as planning change. Since we are never mourning only the current issue, therapy will also help us work on buried issues from the past. Ask yourself, "Is this why losses happen? Is the universe giving me a chance at rising from an ancient tomb?"

Grief must be cold turkey. Alcohol and drugs only distract us from it. "I felt so bad, I took a tranquilizer." The opening clause of that sentence bespeaks grief. The second clause bespeaks the avoidance of grief.

At the end of a relationship, we wonder about our lovability. "He didn't really love me (I now realize)," therefore "I'm unlovable (I blame myself)." Or, "He cannot love anybody (I blame him)."

But how about "I'm lovable; he can love; and he doesn't love me." Adults embrace this more realistic view. Anyone can love. No one is unlovable. Not everyone will love me or will choose to spend their lives with me.

It is common to feel compelled to tell your story to anyone who will listen. This is a normal phase of grief work. Repeating the traumatic details helps you absorb the shock and stress of what occurred. Someday, however, while telling the story of how right you were and how bad she was, you will bore yourself. That is the instinctive signal that the storytelling no longer serves a useful purpose. Then you will stop. With luck, you have enough friends that they are not all worn out from hearing the story again and again by the time you get to that liberating moment!

Someday the other person and the relationship and all that has happened will simply be information for you. That will signal that the grief has run its course and that you have moved on. It takes patience to get there, but you can build patience with practice. Then someone will offhandedly say, "You were both unhappy together, and it had stopped working for you, and now that you are apart, you have a chance at happiness," and the simple honesty of that statement will land inside you with the thud of truth.

Stress obstructs clear thinking. It is wise to declare a moratorium during this time on important financial and legal decisions, relocating, child custody, and so on. It is common during breakups to fantasize about moving away—from the pain. If only it could be that easy! Embarking on any new venture without therapy or feedback from friends at a time like this is dangerous. A good rule may be to have to want something for thirty consecutive days before you decide to proceed with it. This applies especially to getting back together.

The desire for vengeance against the partner who hurt you will probably arise. This is the ego's way of avoiding grief by substituting interaction for inner action—that is, personal work. Allow any feeling or thought, but refrain from acting on it. In the words of an old saying, any bird can fly over your head, but it is up to you whether it builds a nest in your hair.

You may fear that you will never find anyone else or that no one will ever want you. This sort of paranoid delusion is to be dismissed as such, but it also serves the grief work. It prevents you from looking for someone else before you are ready to see who you are.

You may be unable to get the other person or the betrayal out of your mind. The ego prefers to choose one side of a polarity and ignore the other, which helps explain the origin and longevity of obsessive thoughts in which we can focus on only one option. You are not in the control tower. Rather you are challenged to become the landing strip. Simply allow any feelings and thoughts that may safely land or crash on you. They are normal and usually fade with time.

It is a mistake to recontact a former partner too soon. In this instance, it helps to have an ego that is too proud to beg for contact. When is the time right for reconnecting in a friendly way? Probably when you have stopped obsessing and no longer want or need to change him or get even with him. The time for recontact is when you no longer need contact but are ready to normalize relations. That happens when the charge is gone. (Normalizing relations is especially important when you have children's issues to negotiate.)

Grief cannot be willed away. It is best not to attempt to let it go but to let it happen. Allow it—that is, yourself—to take all the time needed, no matter what friends say about how long it is supposed to take to "get over it."

Beware of false hopes that arise when a partner who leaves seems to be on the fence about resuming the relationship. This may not be a sign that she wants to reunite. Ambivalence is normal in any breakup. There are usually many back-and-forth gestures between the statement of an ending and the actual ending. Let time tell you whether there is reasonable hope.

A person who has been left may feel like a little boy with hat in hand, waiting for the other to be kind or to relent and take him back. This is a normal way to feel and can lead to a healthy vulnerability for the future. The psyche has many ways of learning to let go of its hardness and let in the light. At the same time, the little begging boy helps you learn that you have expected too much from other people. Here is a love poem by the Sixth Dalai Lama: "O, I demanded so much of you / In this short lifetime. / Maybe we will find one another again / In the beginning of the next."

"Your wound is beyond healing," said the prophet Jeremiah (30:12). Every grief has an element of inconsolability. There will always be something unresolved, ineradicable in a major loss. Such inconsolability may be familiar from childhood. It is what fuels the longing for the perfect partner. Unfortunately, it often becomes synonymous with a sense of unlovability, so we cannot let in 100 percent of the love that comes our way in adult life.

The scars left by grief can be ugly for years or can heal reasonably well. The outcome depends on the skill of our grief work, just as scars on our body show the varying levels of the skill of the doctors who have treated us over the years.

Let It Bee

JENNIFER LAUCK

A divorce and a bee's nest lead best-selling author Jennifer Lauck to an important lesson in mindfulness. Not everything needs to be fixed or changed; she can embrace the present moment just as it is.

A BUMBLEBEE LIFTS from a hole in the ground. It rises in an unsteady fashion, as if tethered by an invisible wire. The wings move so fast the motion cannot be seen but is rather heard as a humming buzz. The creature makes an adjustment and wobble-flies past my shoulder.

I lean back as it gathers direction and speed. Four-year-old Josephine screams, runs up the porch steps and then into the house. She slams the back door so hard the house quivers. Nine-year-old Spencer hides behind me and grips my arm with such intensity the circulation is cut to my hand.

"Sweetie, my arm," I say.

"Sorry, Mom," Spencer says, easing up his grip.

Another bee lifts out of the hole, the same routine all over again and right behind is another.

We stand on wet grass that is overgrown and lush. I don't mow. Mowing is a man's job and Spencer is too young. Pretty soon, I tell myself, I'll have to get a man or a mower. Or maybe I'll get a gardener.

I shake my arm to get the feeling back and Spencer stands on his toes in order to peek over my shoulder.

"Will they sting us?" Spencer asks.

"Are you covered with pollen?" I put my arm around my son and cup the back of his head with my palm the way I do—something I've done since he was baby. It's our mother-son habit. Our little peculiarity. His head fits my hand perfectly and he wiggles a little as if to nestle in. "Sweets," I say, "bees are not interested in you unless you are a flower."

Two bumblebees return to the hole—lowering their pollen-loaded legs into the ground. Spencer hides his face against my arm and I decide to try humor.

"It's like some kind of bee convention," I say. "Grand Central Bee Terminal. A superpower pollen highway."

Spencer chuckles, which is nice because his father says I don't have a sense of humor. I wish he were here to see how it's not true. I'm funny. I'm hilarious to a nine-year-old.

"I mean, they don't even knock on the door and ask before they take up residence here," I continue. "There is no lease and they don't pay rent. What is the deal?"

Spencer laughs harder still and I roll my eyes with a great show of being outraged. He eases from around my side and goes down on one knee to get a closer look at the bee entry and departure point. The hole, if you weren't looking for it, would be impossible to find. It is no more than the size of a dime with a small rise under the gravel.

"How many live down there?" he asks.

I lift my hands and then let them drop to my sides. "I have no idea." Bee infestation is a man's job, the same as mowing and car maintenance and taking out the trash.

Jo sneaks up behind us and, like her brother a moment ago, she hides behind me.

"Are they gone?" she asks.

"No, honey," I say, "but they aren't going to bother you. They want flowers not little girls."

I put my arm around Jo. She's wearing a pink silk dress over a yellow silk dress over a neon green silk dress. She simply cannot bear to leave one of her princess dresses on a hanger so they are all on her body in layers. Under the dresses, she wears every pair of underwear too. I am thinking she might have been a refugee in a past life.

Two more bumblebees hover around the trunk of the red oak tree—

unsure about a small boy so close to their landing strip. I tap Spencer and point up toward the incoming bees.

On his knees, Spencer isn't sure what I'm trying to say and he moves his head all around. He looks like a dog down there on all fours. When he spots the hovering bees, which are lowering themselves to their home, he yelps. In a flash, both kids run back to the house and it's just me, on the wet grass.

The bees drop to the ground and crawl into their hole.

I've been on my own for nearly a year. Fall, winter, spring, and now summer. It's good. It's right. It's the best thing for me, for my former husband, and for the kids—who didn't deserve to grow up in a home where the big people argued all the time—but it's surprising how many things I delegated to my husband. I just didn't have time or interest in infrastructure. If a wire shorted out or a pipe got clogged or the car needed oil, he was the go-to guy.

If he were here now, he would, without question, have a solution. He would just kill them by dousing the nest with a hose. That's how his own father, a Nebraskan man with a cattle-ranching legacy, would have managed such a pesky situation. Heck, I wouldn't even have been consulted.

But here I am, single—a single mother—and this is what I would call an "infrastructure" issue. I am now the go-to girl.

One of my friends, married to an abusive man, suggests I put a bucket over the hole. She says the bees will likely just move on or die. When things get bad in her marriage, she takes to her bed and hides under the covers for days. She tells her kids that she is sick but she's not. She's depressed.

Another one of my friends, more like an acquaintance, says I should just get some bug spray and let the bees have it. That's what she would do. I have no idea how her marriage is going. We aren't that close.

I have another friend, married to a cop who works the swing shift (meaning she never sees him), and she says that the best way to remove bees is to go out—late at night—and simply ask them to leave in a firm yet loving voice.

"I do this all the time with sugar ants," she says. "And you know what, they just skitter away."

This woman has recently launched a practice as a clairvoyant. She says she can see auras.

• • • • •

For the next few days, I make it a daily practice to study the industry of the bumblebees. After the kids are fed and taken to school, I sit with my elbows on my knees on the bottom step of the back porch, just a few feet south of the nest, and I watch bees lift off, fly over to the hydrangea and beyond, and then return.

Bumblebees, according to the law of aerodynamics, are not supposed to fly. The body is the issue; it's just too big for those tiny wings. And yet, there they go—over and over again. Apparently this is about wing speed. They are the hummingbirds of the insect kingdom. A bumblebee, therefore, defies logic and science.

Online I have discovered that in early Christian traditions, monks lived in beehive-shaped huts, which represented the aim of a harmonious community. The hum sound of chanting is like that hum sound of bee industry.

While I am not a practicing Christian, having set that tradition aside long ago, I am a student of Tibetan Buddhist studies. Each day, I finger prayer beads, read books written by enlightened masters, and even meditate. It's true, there is a hum to my chants of mantra which I accumulate for the benefit of all (which includes bees). I hadn't thought of it that way before.

While my former husband mocks my interest in Buddha, reminding me that I was never spiritual in all the angry years we spent together, I remain focused. Without the constraints of our marriage, I like to think that perhaps I am something like the bumblebee. Meditation, which is—in part—an effort to transcend the human condition of suffering, defies the law of reason and aerodynamics. According to a book I read, *Power verses Force* by David Hawkins, less than half a percent of the human population will achieve transcendent states like pure love. Hawkins also writes that we, as a species, are stuck in the age of reason, meaning that every problem can be rationalized or explained via the mind. Yet, when one transcends to higher states, reason and logic no longer apply.

There is no reason for the bees and yet, as I study them (verses slaughter them), I discover I am the bees and, in an odd way, the bees are me. Perhaps that is why they are here, taking over the backyard.

· · · · ·

"Whatcha doing?" Spencer asks.

He stands at the threshold of the back door and holds a mug in his hand. Hot chocolate. The mug reads *I Love You*. I'm on the bottom step of the back porch with my coffee. There is no message on my mug.

"Just watching the bees," I say.

Spencer pads across the porch and down the steps. He sits on the bottom one and sips at his cocoa. Over the rim, he eyes the hole in the ground. Several bees lift off and fly away.

"They are still here," he points out.

"Indeed," I say.

A gray squirrel jumps from the roof of the garage and into the red oak tree. Spencer points. "A squirrel is just a rat with a good PR campaign," he says, a joke he's heard from his dad and which is actually pretty funny.

"A squirrel is just a rat with a better outfit," I counter and Spencer sputters chocolate in a dramatic spray.

"Oh, that's good," he says using the back of his hand to wipe his mouth.

The squirrel disappears on the other side of the fence and a few bees land on the ground and drop out of sight. I still have no idea how many bees live there, how deep their nest goes, or what they are creating in their dark world but I like to imagine them down there—humming around—following their ancient code.

"Have you decided what to do about them?" Spencer asks. He leans into my side and I put my arm around his lean little boy body. He smells like chocolate and shampoo.

"Obviously not," I say. "They are still with us."

"Well, that's a decision," Spencer points out. "You're letting them stay."

I look down at my son—sweet face, dark eyes, shining hair that is thick and shaped in that popular bowl cut style.

"I guess you're right," I say. "It's the decision to do nothing."

He leans against my shoulder again.

"That's probably fine," he says. "They aren't bothering us."

I move my hand over the back of his head, finding that place where my palm fits so well. He moves his head a little in my hand, as if to nestle in.

PART SIX

Love as a Spiritual Path

Intimate Relationship as a Spiritual Crucible

JOHN WELWOOD

Living with someone we love, with all the joys and challenges, is one of the best ways to grow spiritually. But real awakening only happens, says psychologist John Welwood, in the "charnel ground" where we acknowledge and work with our wounds, fears, and illusions.

WHILE MOST PEOPLE WOULD LIKE to have healthy, satisfying relationships in their lives, the truth is that everyone has a hard time with intimate partnerships. The poet Rilke understood just how challenging they could be when he penned his classic statement, "For one person to love another, this is the most difficult of all our tasks."

Rilke isn't suggesting it's hard to love or to have loving-kindness. Rather, he is speaking about how hard it is to *keep* loving someone we live with, day by day, year after year. After numerous hardships and failures, many people have given up on intimate relationship, regarding the relational terrain as so fraught with romantic illusion and emotional hazards that it is no longer worth the energy.

Although modern relationships are particularly challenging, their very difficulty presents a special arena for personal and spiritual growth. To develop more conscious relationships requires becoming conversant with how three different dimensions of human existence play out within them: ego, person, and being.

Every close relationship involves these three levels of interaction that two partners cycle through—ego to ego, person to person, and being to being. While one moment two people may be connecting being to being in pure openness, the next moment their two egos may fall into deadly combat. When our partners treat us nicely, we open—"Ah, you're so great." But when they say or do something threatening, it's "How did I wind up with you?" Since it can be terribly confusing or devastating when the love of our life suddenly turns into our deadliest enemy, it's important to hold a larger vision that allows us to understand what is happening here.

RELATIONSHIP AS ALCHEMY

When we fall in love, this usually ushers in a special period, one with its own distinctive glow and magic. Glimpsing another person's beauty and feeling, our heart opens in response, providing a taste of absolute love, a pure blend of openness and warmth. This being-to-being connection reveals the pure gold at the heart of our nature, qualities like beauty, delight, awe, deep passion and kindness, generosity, tenderness, and joy.

Yet opening to another also flushes to the surface all kinds of conditioned patterns and obstacles that tend to shut this connection down: our deepest wounds, our grasping and desperation, our worst fears, our mistrust, our rawest emotional trigger points. As a relationship develops, we often find that we don't have full access to the gold of our nature, for it remains embedded in the ore of our conditioned patterns. And so we continually fall from grace.

It's important to recognize that all the emotional and psychological wounding we carry with us from the past is relational in nature: it has to do with not feeling fully loved. And it happened in our earliest relationships—with our caretakers—when our brain and body were totally soft and impressionable. As a result, the ego's relational patterns largely developed as protection schemes to insulate us from the vulnerable openness that love entails. In relationship, the ego acts as a survival mechanism for getting needs met while fending off the threat of being hurt, manipulated, controlled, rejected, or abandoned in ways we were as a child. This is normal and totally understandable. Yet if it's the main tenor of a relationship, it keeps us locked in complex strategies of defensiveness and control that undermine the possibility of deeper connection.

Thus, to gain greater access to the gold of our nature in relationship, a certain alchemy is required: the refining of our conditioned defensive patterns. The good news is that this alchemy generated between two people also furthers a larger alchemy *within* them. The opportunity here is to join and integrate the twin poles of human existence: *heaven,* the vast space of perfect, unconditional openness, and *earth,* our imperfect, limited human form, shaped by worldly causes and conditions. As the defensive/controlling ego cooks and melts down in the heat of love's influence, a beautiful evolutionary development starts to emerge—the genuine person, who embodies a quality of very human relational presence that is transparent to openhearted being, right in the midst of the dense confines of worldly conditioning.

Relationship as Charnel Ground

To clarify the workings of this alchemy, a more gritty metaphor is useful, one that comes from the tantric traditions of Buddhism and Hinduism: relationship as charnel ground. In many traditional Asian societies, the charnel ground was where people would bring dead bodies to be eaten by vultures and jackals. From the tantric yogi's perspective, this was an ideal place to practice, because it is right at the crossroads of life, where birth and death, fear and fearlessness, impermanence and awakening unfold right next to each other. Some things are dying and decaying, others are feeding and being fed, while others are being born out of the decay. The charnel ground is an ideal place to practice because it is right at the crossroads of life, where one cannot help but feel the rawness of human existence.

The Buddhist master Chögyam Trungpa Rinpoche described the charnel ground as "that great graveyard, in which the complexities of samsara and nirvana lie buried." Samsara is the conditioned mind that clouds our true nature, while nirvana is the direct seeing of this nature. Trungpa Rinpoche describes this daunting crossroads in one of his early seminars:

> It's a place to die and be born, equally, at the same time; it's simply our raw and rugged nature, the ground where we constantly puke

and fall down, constantly make a mess. We are constantly dying, we are constantly giving birth. We are eating in the charnel ground, sitting in it, sleeping on it, having nightmares on it. . . . Yet it does not try to hide its truth about reality. There are corpses lying all over the place, loose arms, loose hands, loose internal organs, and flowing hairs all over the place; jackals and vultures are roaming about, each one devising its own scheme for getting the best piece of flesh.

Many of us have a cartoonlike notion of relational bliss: that it should provide a steady state of security or solace that will save us from having to face the gritty, painful, difficult areas of life. We imagine that finding or marrying the right person will spare us from having to deal with such things as loneliness, disappointment, despair, terror, or disintegration. Yet anyone who has been married for a long time probably has some knowledge of the charnel ground quality of relationship—corpses all over the place, and jackals and vultures roaming about looking for the best piece of flesh. Trungpa Rinpoche suggests that if we can work with the "raw and rugged situation" of the charnel ground, "then some spark or sympathy or compassion, some giving in or opening can begin to take place. The chaos that takes place in your neurosis is the only home ground that you can build the mandala of awakening on." This last sentence is a powerful one, for it suggests that awakening happens only through facing the chaos of our neurotic patterns. Yet this is often the last thing we want to deal with in relationships.

Trungpa Rinpoche suggests that our neurosis is built on the fact that

large areas of our life have been devoted to trying to avoid discovering our own experience. Now [in the charnel ground, in our relationships] we have a chance to explore that large area that exists in our being, which we've been trying to avoid. That seems to be the first message, which may be very grim but also very exciting. We're not trying to get away from the charnel ground. We don't want to build a Hilton hotel in the middle of it. Building the mandala of awakening actually happens on the charnel ground. What is happening on the charnel ground is constant personal exploration and, beyond that, just giving, opening, extending yourself completely to the situation that's available to you. Being fantastically exposed and the sense that you could give birth to another world.

This also describes the spiritual potential of intimate involvement with another human being.

Another quote with a similar feeling comes from Swami Rudrananda (a German teacher known as Rudy):

> Don't look for perfection in me. I want to acknowledge my own imperfection; I want to understand that that is part of the endlessness of my growth. It's absolutely useless at this stage in your life, with all of the shit piled up in your closet, to walk around and try to kid yourself about your perfection. Out of the raw material you break down [here he is also speaking of the charnel ground], you grow and absorb the energy. You work yourself from inside out, tearing out, destroying, and finding a sense of nothingness. That nothingness allows God to come in. But this somethingness—ego and prejudices and limitations—is your raw material. If you process and refine it all, you can open consciously. Otherwise, you will never come to anything that represents yourself. . . . The only thing that can create a oneness inside you is the ability to see more of yourself as you work every day to open deeper and say, "Fine, I'm short-tempered," or "Fine, I'm aggressive," or "Fine, I love to make money," or "I have no feeling for anybody else." Once you recognize you're all of these things, you'll finally be able to take a breath and allow these things to open.

Rudy suggests that we have to acknowledge and embrace our imperfections as a spiritual path; therefore, grand spiritual pretensions miss the point. In his words, "A man who thinks he has a spiritual life is really an idiot." The same is true of relationships: beware of thinking you have a "spiritual relationship." While loving connection provides a glimpse of the gold that lies within, we continually corrupt it by turning it into a commodity, a magical charm to make us feel okay. All the delusions of romantic love follow from there. Focusing on relationship as a spiritual or emotional "fix" actually destroys the possibility of finding deep joy, true ease, or honest connection with another.

Sooner or later relationship brings us to our knees, forcing us to confront the raw and rugged mess of our mental and emotional life. George Orwell points to this devastating quality of human love in a sentence that also has a charnel ground flavor to it: "The essence of being human is that one does not seek perfection and that one is prepared, in the end, to be defeated, and broken up by life, which is the inevitable price of fastening one's love upon other human individuals."

This then is the meaning of the charnel ground: we have to be willing to come apart at the seams, to be dismantled, to let our old ego structures fall apart before we can begin to embody sparks of the essential perfection at the core of our nature. To evolve spiritually, we have to allow these unworked, hidden, messy parts of ourselves to come to the surface. It's not that the strategic, controlling ego is something bad or some unnecessary, horrible mistake. Rather, it provides the indispensable grist that makes alchemical transformation possible.

This is not a pessimistic view, because some kind of breakdown is usually necessary before any significant breakthrough into new ways of living not so encumbered by past conditioning. Charnel ground, then, is a metaphor for this breakdown/breakthrough process that is an essential part of human growth and evolution, and one of the gifts of a deep, intimate connection is that it naturally sets this process in motion. Yet no one wants to be dismantled. So there are two main ways that people try to abort this process: running away and spiritual bypassing.

The problem with running away when a relationship becomes difficult is that we are also turning away from ourselves and our potential breakthroughs. Fleeing the raw, wounded places in ourselves because we don't think we can handle them is a form of self-rejection and self-abandonment that turns our feeling body into an abandoned, haunted house. The more we flee our shadowy places, the more they fester in the dark and the more haunted this house becomes. And the more haunted it becomes, the more it terrifies us. This is a vicious circle that keeps us cut off from and afraid of ourselves.

One of the scariest places we encounter in relationship is a deep inner sense of unlove, where we don't know that we're truly lovable just for being who we are, where we feel deficient and don't know our value. This is the raw wound of the heart, where we're disconnected from our true nature, our inner perfection. Naturally we want to do everything we can to avoid this place, fix it, or neutralize it, so we'll never have to experience such pain again.

A second way to flee from the challenges of relationship is through spiritual bypassing—using spiritual ideas or practices to avoid or prematurely transcend relative human needs, feelings, personal issues, and developmental tasks. For example, a certain segment of the contemporary spiritual scene has become infected with a facile brand of "advaita-speak," a one-sided transcendentalism that uses nondual terms and ideas to bypass the challenging work of personal transformation.

Advaita-speak can be very tricky, for it uses absolute truth to disparage relative truth, emptiness to devalue form, and oneness to belittle individuality. The following quotes from two popular contemporary teachers illustrate this tendency: "Know that what appears to be love for another is really love of Self, because other doesn't exist," and "The other's 'otherness' stands revealed as an illusion pertaining to the purely human realm, the realm of form." Notice the devaluation of form and the human realm in the latter statement. By suggesting that only absolute love or being-to-being union is real, these teachers equate the person-to-person element necessary for a transformative love bond with mere ego or illusion.

Yet personal intimacy is a spark flashing out across the divide between self and other. It depends on strong individuals making warm, personal contact, mutually sparking and enriching each other with complementary qualities and energies. This is the meeting of I and Thou, which Martin Buber understood not as an impersonal spiritual union but as a personal communion rooted in deep appreciation of the other's otherness.

A deep, intimate connection inevitably brings up all our love wounds from the past. This is why many spiritual practitioners try to remain above the fray and impersonal in their relationships—so as not to face and deal with their own unhealed relational wounds. But this keeps the wounding unconscious, causing it to emerge as compulsive, shadowy behavior or to dry up passion and juice. Intimate personal connecting cannot evolve unless the old love wounds that block it are faced, acknowledged, and freed up.

As wonderful as moments of being-to-being union can be, the alchemical play of joining heaven and earth in a relationship involves a more subtle and beautiful dance: *not losing our twoness in the oneness, while not losing our oneness in the twoness.* Personal intimacy evolves out of the dancing-ground of dualities: personal and transpersonal, known and unknown, death and birth, openness and karmic limitation, clarity and chaos, hellish clashes and heavenly bliss. The clash and interplay of these polarities, with all their shocks and surprises, provide a ferment that allows for deep transformation through forcing us to keep waking up, dropping preconceptions, expanding our sense of who we are, and learning to work with all the different elements of our humanity.

When we're in the midst of this ferment, it may seem like some kind of fiendish plot. We finally find someone we really love, and then the most difficult things start emerging: fear, distrust, unlove, disillusion, resentment, blame, confusion. Yet this is a form of love's grace—that it brings our wounds and defenses forward into the light. For love can only heal what presents itself to be healed. If our woundedness remains hidden, it cannot be healed; the best in us cannot come out unless the worst comes out as well.

So instead of constructing a fancy hotel in the charnel ground, we must be willing to come down and relate to the mess on the ground. We need to regard the wounded heart as a place of spiritual practice. This kind of practice means engaging with our relational fears and vulnerabilities in a deliberate, conscious way, like the yogis of old who faced down the goblins and demons of the charnel grounds.

The only way to be free of our conditioned patterns is through a full, conscious experience of them. This might be called "ripening our karma," what the Indian teacher Swami Prajnanpad described as *bhoga,* meaning "deliberate, conscious experience." He said, "You can only dissolve karma through the bhoga of this karma." We become free of what we're stuck in only through meeting and experiencing it directly. Having the bhoga of your karma allows you to digest unresolved, undigested elements of your emotional experience from the past that are still affecting you: how you were hurt or overwhelmed, how you defended yourself against that by shutting down, how you constructed walls to keep people out.

Another term for directly engaging our karma might be "conscious suffering." This involves saying yes to our pain, opening ourselves to it, as it is. This kind of yes doesn't mean, "I like it, I'm glad it's like this." It just means, "Yes, this is what's happening." Whatever comes up, you are willing to meet it and have a direct experience of it. For example, if you're hard-hearted, you have a full experience of that. Then you see how acknowledging this affects you and what comes from doing that.

Bhoga involves learning to ride the waves of our feelings rather than becoming submerged in them. This requires mindfulness of where we are in the cycle of emotional experience. A skilled surfer is aware of exactly where he is on a wave, whereas an unskilled surfer winds up getting creamed. By their very nature, waves are rising 50 percent of the time and falling the other 50 percent. Instead of fighting the down cycles of our emotional life, we need to learn to keep our seat on the surfboard and have a full, conscious experience of going down. Especially in a culture that is addicted to "up," we especially need our yes when the down cycles unfold— to be willing to fall apart, retreat, slow down, be patient, let go. For it's often at the bottom of a down cycle, when everything looks totally bleak and miserable, that we finally receive a flash of insight that lets us see the hidden contours of some huge ego fixation in which we've been stuck all our life. Having a full, conscious experience of the down cycle as it's occurring, instead of fighting or transcending it, lets us be available for these moments of illumination.

While the highlands of absolute love are most beautiful, few but the saints can spend all their time there. Relative human love is not a peak experience or a steady state. It wavers, fluctuates, waxes and wanes, changes shape and intensity, soars and crashes. "This is the exalted melancholy of our fate," writes Buber, describing how moments of I/Thou communion cannot last too very long. Yet though relationships participate fully in the law of impermanence, the good news is that this allows new surprises and revelations to keep arising endlessly.

Relationship as Koan

Relating to the full spectrum of our experience in the relational charnel ground leads to a self-acceptance that expands our capacity to embrace and accept others as well. Usually our view of our partners is colored by what they do for us—how they make us look or feel good, or not—and shaped by our internal movie about what we want them to be. This, of course, makes it hard to see them for who they are in their own right.

Beyond our movie of the other is a much larger field of personal and spiritual possibilities, what Walt Whitman referred to when he said, "I contain multitudes." These multitudes are what keep a relationship fresh and interesting, but they can only do that if we can accept the ways that those we love are different from us—in their background, values, perspectives, qualities, sensitivities, preferences, ways of doing things, and finally, their destiny. In the words of Swami Prajnanpad, standing advaita-speak on its head, "To see fully that the other is not you is the way to realizing oneness. . . . Nothing is separate, everything is different. . . . Love is the appreciation of difference."

Two partners not holding themselves separate, while remaining totally distinct—"not two, not one"—may seem like an impossible challenge in a relationship. Bernard Phillips, an early student of East/West psychology, likens this impossibility of relationship to a Zen koan, a riddle that cannot be solved with the conceptual mind. After continually trying and failing to figure out the answer, Zen students arrive at a genuine solution only in the moment of finally giving up and giving in. In Phillips's words,

> Every human being with whom we seek relatedness is a koan, that is to say, an impossibility. There is no formula for getting along with a human being. No technique will achieve relatedness. I am impossible to get along with; so is each one of you; all our friends are impossible; the members of our families are impossible. How then shall we get along with them? . . . If you are seeking a real encounter, then you must confront the koan represented by the other person. The koan is an invitation to enter into reality.

In the end, to love another requires dropping all our narcissistic agendas, movies, hopes, and fears, so that we may look freshly and see "the raw other, the sacred other," just as he or she is. This involves a surrender, or perhaps defeat, as in George Orwell's words about being "defeated and broken up by life." What is defeated here, of course, is the ego and its strategies, clearing the way for the genuine person to emerge, the person who is capable of real, full-spectrum contact. The nobility of this kind of defeat is portrayed by Rilke in four powerful lines describing Jacob's wrestling match with the angel:

Winning does not tempt that man
For this is how he grows:
By being defeated, decisively,
By constantly greater beings.

In relationship, it is two partners' greater beings, gradually freeing themselves from the prison of conditioned patterns, that bring about this decisive defeat. And as this starts reverberating through their relationship, old expectations finally give way, old movies stop running, and a much larger acceptance than they believed possible can start opening up between them. As they become willing to face and embrace whatever stands between them—old relational wounds from the past, personal pathologies, difficulties hearing and understanding each other, different values and sensitivities—all in the name of loving and letting be, they are invited to "enter into reality." Then it becomes possible to start encountering each other nakedly, in the open field of nowness, fresh and unfabricated, the field of love forever vibrating with unimagined possibilities.

Marriage as a Path of Compassion

RICHARD BOROFSKY

A psychotherapist specializing in couples' therapy, Richard Borofsky shares his views on what a precious opportunity marriage affords us. Over time, he says, it enables us to see the limits of our compassion and to expand those limits.

OVER TWENTY-FIVE YEARS AGO I became a student of Rinzai Zen master Joshu Sasaki-roshi. In Rinzai Zen, teachers use koans, which are questions that cannot be answered conceptually or with words. They can only be answered by manifesting an enlightened presence. Thus, it is not uncommon for a student to work on a particular koan for several years before a Zen master "passes" the student. Among the first koans my teacher gave me was, "How do you realize your true nature when you are with your wife?" The words *true nature* in this koan refer to the awakened, enlightened state, or buddha nature. So this koan was an invitation to manifest my buddha nature *while* being with my wife. Or more simply, it was an invitation to become an awakened, enlightened husband—a husband who is a buddha.

It has been several years since I was given this koan, and I am not yet a buddha-husband. I am merely an *apprentice* buddha-husband. This is good, because committed relationships insist, above all, on humility. I no longer expect to graduate from my apprenticeship or to receive some sort of diploma. It wouldn't matter if I did. Diplomas from the University of Love and Marriage tend to be obsolete within a very few days.

What has happened during all these years, though, is that I have come to see marriage as a kind of spiritual curriculum with a major in compassion. And I would like to offer you the benefit and merit of what I have learned from walking, waltzing, traipsing, and trudging along this marathon path of matrimony.

First of all, and most important, I've learned that marriage, like most things in life, works better the more awareness I have. By "awareness," I mean the innate capacity we all have to notice—ourselves, others, and the environment. Our awareness is an unwavering, unblinking witness; it is an omnipresent presence, perfectly impersonal, impartial as a star, without will or volition, silently and serenely assenting to everything. This is our true nature, our buddha nature, our essential being. This is what makes love, compassion, and relationship possible.

Unfortunately, for most of us, this capacity for awareness is severely obscured by the compulsive activity of our minds. These activities include constant monitoring of the multimedia attractions and distractions of our everyday experience (sensations, sights, sounds, feelings, and thoughts); seeking stimulation and satisfaction; trying to know and understand what's going on; explaining the past; planning, predicting, and controlling the future; and resisting any diminishment to our self-image.

It is only when this activity of mind subsides and the light of our awareness is apparent that we can relate to each other authentically and compassionately. In the light of present awareness, we can find each other, see each other clearly, and be together in the place that we always are—right here. *Here* you are! *Here* I am! *Here we are!* And being here together with awareness, we are able to wholeheartedly immerse ourselves in whatever experience our life together has to offer. Now we are one—wonderfully, *onefully* together. Now we are two—a separate "me" and "you," a kiss or a collision of differences. By turns, our being together may be blissful, funny, angry, tender, hurtful, or healing. It is continuously and kaleidoscopically changing. By witnessing *as* we experience all these changes, gradually, palpably, compassion appears. Being aware and present, we gradually wake up together to our common humanity and to something larger than ourselves.

Being aware and present, we also discover that we have no alternative but to accept each other and what is happening between us right now. That is because what is happening between us is *already* in play. Perhaps in the next moment we will say or do something that could change our relationship for the better. But nothing we say or do will be successful if it does not involve a full acceptance of this present actuality. This is because authentic change requires that we see and accept where we are. We must start *here*. Especially in relationships, resisting or trying to change what is happening *now* actually prevents change from happening later. Compulsively contriving to manipulate and change each other is what keeps relationships stuck.

If we can stay present, accepting whatever is happening on its own terms, we often discover to our surprise that, paradoxically, the changes we most deeply desired in ourselves or in our partners are occurring spontaneously. We see that happiness and love can appear naturally—like sunshine, like snow, like spring. So can pain. Part of compassion is being able to allow things to happen on their own terms, despite our preferences. The Third Chinese Zen patriarch, Seng-t'san, wrote, "The great way is not difficult for those who have no preferences." This is probably nowhere more true than in intimate partnerships.

Of course, most of us are not prepared to practice this kind of radical acceptance. We have very strong preferences about the kind of experiences we want to be having, and we are not about to relinquish them. We find it difficult to accept that relationships involve such a mix of positive and negative experiences. Most of us enter into relationship in order to find comfort, a refuge, a safe harbor to get away from the storms of the world. What we discover, to our dismay, is that our intimate relationships are just as mixed and messy as anything out there in the world. We discover that the safe harbor sometimes becomes a storm itself. We find ourselves, as Pablo Neruda describes it in one of his love sonnets, "in the land of kisses and volcanoes."

Rather than accept this, we look for an alternative, the way we might if we were watching television. If we don't like what we are seeing on TV, we reach for the remote control and switch to another channel. Similarly, if we don't like our experience in being with another, we tend to assume that it could be, indeed *should* be, changed. When something unpleasant or painful arises, we make every effort to change it. If that fails, we console ourselves with trying to understand what is *wrong* with ourselves or our partner or our relationship. And if that fails, we are left to ponder the possibility that this match, which seemed "made in heaven," was an illusion.

In the everyday life of relationship, in so many different ways, we are trying to have reality be other than how it is.

The fact is, if we're honest, relationships are often extremely painful. For many of us, the greatest pain of our lives has occurred with an intimate partner. This needs to be acknowledged. It also needs to be understood. We need to ask ourselves, why is this the nature of relationships? Is it because we are incompetent at relating and loving? Is it because we all have the wrong partners and need to exchange them for others who are more compatible? Or is it rather because there is something about relationships that we have fundamentally missed or misunderstood? This last explanation, I think, is the most useful. I think we have indeed missed the essential point or purpose of being together in a long-term intimate relationship.

For me, the deepest purpose of a committed relationship is to cultivate compassion. Compassion in a relationship does not exclude positive experiences, and certainly it does not exclude love. It is just very much larger than any of these experiences. Indeed, compassion, as I am using the word, includes *everything* that is part of our collective experience: heartbreak that brings us to our knees, overflowing fulfillment, boredom, bedlam, deep peace of mind, anxiety, transcendent sex, helpless rage, jubilant reunions, and eventual death, to name just a few of the possibilities. In other words, I am suggesting that compassion is quite a human stew. The recipe includes everything, including considerable quantities of pain, all folded into immeasurable amounts of love, mindfully stirred over a low heat with grandmotherly good humor and a wisdom that can always glimpse a bigger picture. This is what makes compassion really cook.

What I'm suggesting here is an approach to relationship that values compassion above feelings of comfort and love and requires a disciplined, dedicated effort to stay open to the mixed and metamorphosing reality of *all* our moments together. In a word, this is a practice of saying yes—yes to every eventuality. Yes to the sweet ease of lying together, to the poignancy of our missings and misunderstandings, to our vagaries and vulnerabilities and laughter; yes to surprises (both pleasing and painful); yes to our prodigal losses and our prolific fears; yes to familiarity and comfort. Yes to everything.

We say yes because, when compassion is unqualified and unconditional, *nothing* is excluded. Approached in this way, relationship is a practice of opening over and over again to the whole human condition as it manifests in the crucible of our intimate, committed partnership. Approached in this way, our relationship becomes a kind of compassion factory, converting everything that happens into a whole and openhearted *humankindness.*

Because it is easy to misunderstand, I want to clarify what I mean by "saying yes to everything." I am *not* advocating that we passively accept unwholesome, harmful, unjust, or abusive situations or that we forswear using the word *no* when it is necessary. What I am suggesting is that all our negative feelings—such as hatred, grief, shame, and terror—can all be used in the service of compassion if we hold these experiences together in the light of our present awareness rather than trying to escape from them, which inevitably makes things worse. The word *compassion* means literally "to be in pain together." In other words, your pain is part of my experience, and my pain is part of yours. There is no escape. Any attempt to escape from your pain or mine is futile. Like trying to escape from quicksand, we will only sink deeper into it.

I'm saying that the only way to "get out of" the unavoidable painful and negative experiences that occur in relationship is to transform them into compassion. This happens when we say yes. This yes does *not* mean that I condone or like what is happening. It simply means that I accept that this pain and negativity exist and that they exist in us and in our relationship. We are not trying to eliminate them. Rather, we are enfolding them into a larger lovingness, an aware presence, symbolized by the word *yes.* When we say yes, there is an alchemy that happens, which can transform even the most extreme negativity into compassion.

There is a transmutation that happens when we are willing to know the full depth of our collective sorrow, and this is how suffering becomes kindness. Learning to make this transmutation is, I believe, the essential challenge of an enduring intimate relationship. This is what is implied in the vows that most married couples take at their wedding ceremony. The vows usually go something like this: "Do you take this man or woman to be the companion of your heart, to have and to hold from this day forth, for better or for worse, for richer or for poorer, in sickness or in health, as long as you both shall live?" Of course, the expected answer is yes. But we have no idea, really, what we are saying yes to. This yes is untested. We do not know yet the limits of our capacity to accept all the different circumstances that will occur in our life together. We will find out in time. This is the great opportunity that marriage affords—to enable us, over time, to see the limits of our compassion and to keep expanding these limits. I know of no other endeavor that can do this so powerfully—if we accept the challenge. To do this, we only need to be sure that, whatever may happen to us, *yes* is always the *last* word we say.

The poet Wallace Stevens said it succinctly: "After the final no, there comes a yes / And on that yes, the future world depends." On that yes also depends the possibility of a committed, compassionate intimacy.

May All Beings Be Happy

Joseph Goldstein

Most of us believe that we can feel deep love for only one person—or maybe a handful of people at best. But, says Joseph Goldstein, Insight Meditation Society cofounder, with loving-kindness, our love can grow to embrace the entire world.

THE SANSKRIT WORD *maitri* and the Pali word *metta* both mean "loving-kindness" or "loving care" and refer to an attitude of friendliness, goodwill, and generosity of heart. When we are filled with loving-kindness and a sense of loving care, we have a very simple wish: May all beings be happy.

This kind of love has many qualities that distinguish it from our more usual experiences of love mixed with desire or attachment. Born of great generosity, metta is a caring and kindness that does not seek self-benefit. It does not look for anything in return or by way of exchange: "I will love you if you love me," or "I will love you if you behave a certain way." Because loving-kindness is never associated with anything harmful, it always arises from a purity of heart.

One of the unique aspects of metta is that it does not make distinctions among beings. When we feel love mixed with desire, this feeling is always for a limited number of people. We may love and desire one person, or maybe two or three at a time, or maybe several in series. But does anyone in this world *desire* all beings?

Loving-kindness, on the other hand, is extraordinary precisely because it can embrace all; there is no one who falls outside of its domain. That is why, when we encounter people who have developed this capacity to a great extent—the Dalai Lama, for example—we sense their tremendous kindness toward everyone. Loving-kindness is a feeling that blesses others and oneself with the simple wish, "Be happy." The Japanese poet Issa expresses this openhearted feeling so well: "In the cherry blossom's shade, there's no such thing as a stranger."

Although we may not always live in a steady state of loving feeling, through practice, we can learn to touch it many times a day.

The Practice of Loving-Kindness for Oneself

One way to develop and strengthen metta within us is through the following specific meditation practice, which we start by extending loving feelings toward ourselves.

It's very simple. At first, just sit in some comfortable position, and keeping an image or felt sense of yourself in mind, slowly repeat phrases of loving-kindness for yourself: *"May I be happy, may I be peaceful, may I be free of suffering."* Say these or any other phrases that reflect feelings of care and well-wishing over and over again. We do this not as an affirmation, but rather as an expression of a caring *intention*. As you repeat the words, focus the mind on this intention of kindness; it slowly grows into a powerful force in your life.

Although the practice is straightforward, at times it can be extremely difficult. As you turn your attention inward and send loving wishes toward yourself, you might see a considerable amount of self-judgment or feelings of unworthiness. At these times, proceed gently, as if you were holding a young child. A line from an old Japanese samurai poem expresses well this part of the practice: "I make my mind my friend."

The Practice of Loving-Kindness for a Benefactor

After strengthening feelings of loving-kindness for ourselves, we then send these very same wishes to a benefactor, someone who has aided us in some way in our lives. This might be a parent, a teacher, or even someone we don't know personally but whose life has nonetheless had a positive influence on our own. One person who was having difficulty connecting with loving-kindness said that she opened to the feeling of metta most easily when she thought of her dog—a being who always gave her unquestioning love. Benefactors can take many forms.

In this part of the practice, hold the image or sense of that person (or other being) in your mind, as if you were talking directly to them, and then direct your intention of metta toward him or her: *"Be happy, be peaceful, be free of suffering."*

This stage is often easier than directing metta toward ourselves, because we usually already have warm and caring feelings for those who have helped us.

THE PRACTICE OF LOVING-KINDNESS FOR ALL

From a benefactor, we move on to other categories of people. We send loving wishes to loved ones who are very close to us personally; then to those who are neutral, about whom we have no strong feelings one way or another; and then to "enemies" or difficult people. Finally, we send loving-kindness to all beings everywhere.

It's important to move through this progression at your own speed. There is no timetable. Some categories may be easier than others. Whenever you feel that you're able to generate genuine feelings of loving care for one, move on to the next.

This can be practiced intensively in the solitude of a meditation retreat, in our daily practice at home, or even as we're walking down the street or driving to work. In all cases, it begins to change how we relate to others in the world.

As an experiment, the next time you are doing an errand, are stuck in traffic, or are standing in line at the supermarket, instead of being preoccupied with where you're going or what needs to be done, take a moment to simply send loving wishes to all those around you. Often, there is an immediate and very remarkable shift inside as we feel more connected and more present.

When I first began the practice of metta, I had an experience that revealed a lot about my mind and the way I was relating to others. At the time, I was developing loving-kindness toward a neutral person—although I wasn't really sure what a "neutral person" meant. My teacher, Anagarika

Munindra, simply said to pick someone nearby for whom I didn't have much feeling one way or another.

I was in India at the time, and there was an old gardener at the little monastery where I was staying. I saw him every day, but I had never really given him any thought at all. He was just somebody I noticed in passing. It was quite startling to realize how many such people there were around me, beings for whom I had completely neutral feelings. That in itself was an illuminating discovery.

So every day for weeks, I began visualizing this old gardener in my meditation, repeating phrases like "May you be happy, may you be peaceful, may you be free from suffering." After a while, I began to feel great warmth and caring for him, and every time we passed, my heart just opened.

This was a great turning point in my practice. I understood that how I feel about someone is up to me and that my feelings do not ultimately depend on the person, his or her behavior, or the situation. The gardener remained the same. He did not change what he was doing or how he related to me. But because of a turn in my own understanding and practice, my heart began to fill with genuine feelings of kindness and care.

That's the Power of Love

THE FOURTEENTH DALAI LAMA

The Dalai Lama explains that even just one person with a warm heart can make the world a better place.

AS HUMAN BEINGS, we are basically all the same; after all, we all belong to the same planet. All sentient beings have the same innate nature that wants happiness and doesn't want to suffer. All of us love ourselves and desire something good. Now, as far as material development is concerned, we have already achieved a great deal, and every nation on this planet is aiming for better facilities and is attempting to create a more prosperous society.

Eventually we may achieve that. However, material development alone is not sufficient for human happiness. The reason is quite simple: human beings are not the product of a machine; we are something more. Therefore, we need more than just external objects in order to be happy.

The most important thing in life is human affection. Without it, one cannot achieve genuine happiness. And if we want a happier life, a happier family, happier neighbors, or a happier nation, the key is inner quality. Even if the five billion human beings who inhabit the earth become millionaires, without inner development there cannot be peace or any lasting happiness. Some people may be very rich, but we often find that they are not happy at all. Affection, love, and compassion are some of the most important elements in our life. Peace of mind is crucial for good health. Of course, good facilities, the right medicine, and food also make a difference. But happiness is the most important factor for good health.

Everybody is concerned about world peace. Weapons or military force, under certain circumstances at certain times, can produce some relative peace. In the long run, however, it is impossible to achieve genuine and lasting world peace through military confrontation or hatred and suspicion. World peace must develop through mental peace, mutual trust, and mutual respect. For that, again, compassion or altruistic mind is the key factor.

Let us consider the significance of a happy family. The most important thing is affection. Whether we are successful in life or not depends a lot on the atmosphere we grow up in. Children from families full of love and compassion are happier and more successful human beings. On the other hand, a child's life may be ruined if he or she grows up in fear or lacks love and affection.

Where does affection come from, and how can one develop or increase human affection? So long as the human mind exists, the seed of affection exists. Although negative and positive thoughts and emotions are all part of the human mind, the dominant force in human consciousness or human life is affection. Therefore, the seed of compassion is a part of one's nature right from birth. When we are born, we are free from all ideology and religion that come later, but we are not free from the need for human affection. A baby cannot survive without it.

Affection is an important element in conception. Human affection and compassion are not just about love or seeking pleasure. True compassion is not only about sympathy or a feeling of closeness, but a sense of responsibility as well. Genuine compassion is generated when we realize that people who suffer or lack happiness or prosperity want happiness just like us. Compassion is about developing genuine concern for them.

Usually we think of compassion as a feeling of closeness toward our friends, but that is a view tainted by mental projections. As long as a person is a close friend, we have a positive attitude toward him or her. As soon as that person's attitude changes or as soon as our feelings toward that person change, compassion ceases to exist as well. This is not really compassion, but more of an attachment.

Genuine compassion involves analyzing the situation regardless of whether the person is close or not. The fact remains that the person has a problem and is suffering and has the same right as I do to overcome the suffering and to be happy.

Marriage and conception are not results of mad love alone. They come of knowing each other well. When you know your partner's mental attitude as well as his or her physical aspect, you can develop mutual trust and respect. It is only on that basis that marriage can take place. There is a sense of responsibility involved. Human conception should take place under such circumstances.

As human beings, we have intelligence and extraordinary abilities. Those who have more intelligence are more farsighted, and those who are more able also have a greater responsibility toward themselves as well as others. In fact, human beings are responsible not only for other human beings but for the well-being of other sentient beings and our planet as well. If we utilize our intelligence and abilities in a destructive manner, it will result in disaster and tragedy. We must utilize them constructively instead. I am quite sure that those with extraordinary intelligence and ability who manipulate other people or things for their own benefit end up having some deep regret.

I think that both humans and animals have an innate appreciation for truth. If we treat dogs or cats sincerely, they appreciate it. If we cheat them, they realize that and don't like it. If one human being communicates truthfully with another, it is appreciated. If we cheat others, they will react accordingly, whether they are believers or nonbelievers, rich or poor, educated or uneducated. Therefore, compassion and honesty exist because we don't want to cheat people and because we all have the same right to be happy. Compassion, as I mentioned earlier, is a combination of sympathy and concern, a feeling of closeness with a sense of responsibility.

Some people feel that compassion, love, and forgiveness are religious matters. This is wrong. Love and compassion are imperative. There is no way one can ignore these things, whether one is a believer or not. They are necessary if we want happiness and if we want to be good citizens. As far as religion is concerned, if accepting a particular religion makes you comfortable, then you should take up that religion. If you do not want to, it doesn't matter; leave it. But it is important to understand the nature of compassion, because it is a basic and necessary human quality.

Happiness is mental. Machines cannot provide us with it, nor can we buy it. Money and wealth are only partial sources of happiness, not happiness per se. These will not produce happiness directly. Happiness must develop within ourselves; nobody can give it to us. Its ultimate source is tranquillity or peace of mind. It doesn't depend on external factors. It doesn't matter if we lack good facilities, a good education, or a successful life, as long as we have inner confidence.

Concern and regard for others, and human affection, are extremely important factors for our happiness. Compassion gives us inner strength, a feeling of inner value.

Try to become a good human being with a warm heart, regardless of whether you are a politician, a religious person, a businessperson, or whatever. One's individual behavior can contribute to the making of a happier family and community.

Searching for the Heart of Compassion

Marc Ian Barasch

Call it love, kindness, compassion for all beings—it's the real elixir, the only one that truly transforms life for ourselves and others. We all know that, every religion says it, but where do we find it? Author and environmental activist Marc Ian Barasch searches for compassion in action, compassionate people, and ways to find compassion inside himself.

Every now and then, I'll meet an escapee, someone who has broken free of self-centeredness and lit out for the territory of compassion. You've met them too, those people who seem to emit a steady stream of, for want of a better word, love vibes. As soon as you come within range, you feel embraced, accepted for who you are. For those of us who suspect that you rarely get something for nothing, such geniality can be discomfiting: *They don't even know me. It's just generic cornflakes.* But it feels so good to be around them. They stand there, radiating photons of goodwill, and despite yourself, you beam back, and the world, in a twinkling, changes.

I appreciate these compassionmongers, even marvel at them. I rarely think that I could be like them. Sure, I've tried to live a benign life, putting my shoulder to the wheel for peace, justice, and Mother Earth (mostly churning out words on a page, bouncing signals off the satellites). I doubt that it's made me much less egotistical (maybe a bit more so). I still have that too-cool objectivity that can suck away my sympathies like an outgoing tide.

But I want to be good. Not that cramped, chiding Moral Majority good (I'll keep my minority status, thanks). Not sticky sweet, watch-your-insulin-level good. Just deep-down, unfailingly kind. The fact that I'm not, when the world could use so much more kindness, frankly vexes my spirit.

Oh, I'm a nice enough guy. Like most people, I adore my offspring, even when they drive me crazy; love my parents, despite the corkscrew of childhood; dote on my siblings (though there is that scrapbook of old slights); treasure my friends (even if they sometimes let me down). Conventional wisdom wouldn't fault me for saving the best stuff for my nearest and dearest and giving the rest of humanity the leftovers.

Thus it is, say the sages, that the harvest of kindness—of kindredness—is winnowed down to a precious few grains. For at the center of all spiritual traditions is the beacon of a truly radical proposal: open your heart to everybody. *Everybody.*

What is compassion, that X factor that every faith (the founders, if not the followers) exalts as a supreme virtue? When the Dalai Lama says, "My only religion is kindness," and the pope calls for a "civilization of love," it can't be just mealymouthed piety. Kindness and love are powers unto themselves, able to transmute even the most relentless enmity. Nelson Mandela once remarked that he befriended his jailers, those grim, khaki-clad overseers of his decades of hard labor in a limestone quarry, by "exploiting their good qualities." Asked if he believed all people were kind at their core, he responded, "There is no doubt whatsoever, provided you are able to arouse their inherent goodness." If that sounds like wishful thinking, well, he actually did it.

When I was in my twenties, my Buddhist teacher tricked me into taking a vow of universal compassion. Using some spiritual sleight of hand I've yet to unravel, he made it seem I could aspire to a tender concern for everybody, even putting their welfare before my own.

Fat chance, I'd thought. But in his wily way, he had framed this vow—the bodhisattva's promise to live for others—as a case of enlightened self-interest. It was not, he told me, a matter of wearing a one-size-fits-all hair shirt. I was taking the vow for my own good. It would give me some leverage to pry loose, finger by finger, the claustrophobic monkey-grip of ego; give the heart a little breathing room. By treating others generously, I might find them responding in kind. I felt I was being made privy to an ancient secret: *To attain your own human potential, be mindful of everyone else's.*

At some point in my vow ceremony, a deceptively casual affair held in a rocky field, it *had* felt as if my vision suddenly cleared. I'd glimpsed, like a sky swept clean of clouds, everyone's innate okayness. Years later, I still marveled at the spiritual chutzpah of the liturgy: *However innumerable are beings, I vow to save them all.* It was vintage Buddhist bravado—a pledge to empty all the world's oceans using only an eyedropper. Hardly knowing what I was doing, I had planted myself in a millennia-old tradition that claims you can love all without preconditions, exclusionary clauses or bottom lines; that says life isn't *quid pro quo*, but *quid pro bono*.

To my surprise, the vow hadn't made me feel obligated, but liberated from my own suffocating strictures, from the narrowness of my concerns. It was as if I'd been waiting for a signal, a green light to step onto the crosswalk to the opposite curb; some goad to be compassionate not out of blind craving for virtue, but because it seemed the only genuinely interesting thing to do with my life.

Just forming the intention to make myself useful felt salutary, like some fast-acting antivenin to my snakebit business as usual. I had assumed life was about magnifying myself (for the greater good, of course), but now that seemed like the wrong end of the telescope: It made everyone else look small. I soon took a job running a residential therapeutic community in exchange for room and board, surprised at my ability to care for the walking wounded. I stopped thinking so much about how others had let me down, broken my heart, failed to anticipate my needs or take my oh-so unique sensitivities into account. I began striving to see—and even nourish—other people's possibilities, receiving in return those surprise concoctions that the human spirit dishes out when it feels accepted and at its ease.

But there came a point on my journey when I'd stumbled badly and fell far: a dire illness, an interminable recovery, penury, loneliness, full-on despair. Friends clucked in sympathy but stepped gingerly over the body. Family didn't do much better. I had a soul-curdling realization: the people you love (and who ostensibly love you) may not be there when you need them most. I got through it—the kindness of strangers and all—but I was soon back to squinting at people through my cool fish eye, seeing their preening vanity, their intellectual shortfalls, their ethical squishiness. It took time until I realized such shortsightedness takes a toll—let alone that there was anything I could do about it.

Finding my way back to meditation helped. Nothing like getting a good, long look at myself (and funny how much I looked like everyone else). I noticed how often my social trade-offs were more about getting than giving, how many of *my* thoughts revolved in geosynchronous orbit around Planet Numero Uno. Inner work is a warts-and-all proposition; it gets harder to kid yourself. Still, my teacher had insisted one thing was certain: despite seeing all the ego's pitfalls and pratfalls, real bodhisattvas make friends with themselves. Everyone, he said, possessed some worth past quantifying or qualifying, some value beyond judgment or fine-tuning—and that included oneself.

To love our neighbor as ourselves, after all, is the great injunction of every religion. But what does loving yourself *mean*? It's one thing to say it, another to know it in your bones. Do I talk to the mirror, whispering sweet nothings, tenderly imagine a little homunculus inside me and pet it, tickle it, scratch it behind the ears? The spiritual consensus seems to be that it's like learning to love anyone: you start by getting to know them. The side benefit to this is that to know yourself is also to know the person sitting next to you and the one halfway around the world. "Read thyself," wrote philosopher Thomas Hobbes. "Whosoever looketh into himself . . . shall know what are the thoughts and passions of other men."

Still, having looketh'd into myself, I can't say I loveth all I see. I *have* read myself, and there in oversize type, it says, "petty, suspicious, greedy, vain, jealous, lazy, stingy, dull" (and that's just on the page; there's more between the lines). That I also reckon myself to be magnanimous, conscientious, loyal, thrifty, brave, and intermittently humble is beside the point. It's not enough to offset scourging self-judgment with a roll call of compensating pluses. We have to take ourselves (and each other) whole. The Dalai Lama points out that the Tibetan term for compassion, *tsewa,* generally means "love of others," but "one can have that feeling toward oneself as well. It is a state of mind where you extend how you relate to yourself toward others." If it's true that what goes around comes around, compassion is about nothing if not love's tendency to circulate.

And radiate. Alexander Pope (poet of the "eternal sunshine of the spotless mind") envisioned compassion as a series of concentric circles rippling outward:

Self-love but serves the virtuous mind to wake,
As the small pebble stirs the peaceful lake;

. . . .

Friend, parent, neighbor, first it will embrace;
His country next; and next all human race.

It sounds great. It *is* great. But for many of us, there's a nagging doubt that this whole compassion routine could edge into self-effacement—into loving others *instead* of ourselves, giving away the store until our shelves are bare. The usual formula is first to stockpile some extra self-esteem, *then* you can afford to be generous. That isn't quite how the nineteenth-century religious philosopher Søren Kierkegaard saw it. The command to love thy neighbor, he wrote, had but one purpose: "as with a pick, [to] wrench open the lock of self-love and wrest it away from a person." (He said it approvingly, but . . . oh, great, now compassion will *burglarize* us.) What about looking out for number one? Isn't it prudent to follow that flight attendant's advisory: "First place the mask over your own nose and mouth, tightening the straps to begin the flow of oxygen?" We're of no use to anyone if we're passed out in our seat from hypoxia.

It's a hard balance to strike. If I am not for myself, who will be? But if I am only for myself, what am I? There is a growing sense in our society— left, right, and center—that the balance has woozily tipped, that our obsession with seamless self-contentment ("What I love about Subway is it's all about *me!*") has occluded our ability to love each other. Our cultural default setting has become "get your own needs met." Our psychosocial mean temperature, suggested one recent article, is "people-friendly narcissism." Our therapeutic model focuses so much on strengthening the ego-self that it omits what some dissident psychologists call the self-in-relation. One group of mostly female psychologists has proposed "openness to mutual influence" as a more reliable barometer of mental health than self-esteem.

But *self-esteem* is our all-purpose buzzword, a stock phrase in therapists' offices, corporate training modules, even elementary school curricula. This is fine on the face of it; after all, what's the alternative— self-loathing? Psychologist Abraham Maslow coined the term itself in 1940 after observing a monkey colony in a Madison, Wisconsin, zoo. He was fascinated by the cockiness of the troupe's dominant alphas and the social benefits they accrued, so reminiscent of socially successful people. His concept of self-esteem, then, had its origin not as simple self-affirmation, but as the alpha's great cry of triumphal self-love: I *Am* Somebody—and You're Not. (Maslow's first stab at a terminology was "dominance-feeling.") This self-esteem was more akin to that sense of self that made Sinatra sing about how swell it was to be king of the hill.

What Maslow failed to stress was the social dimension. Even in a primate colony—especially so—no ape is an island. Modern primatologists point out that an alpha animal, contrary to its reputation as solitary lord of all it surveys, is thickly enmeshed in a social webbing, dependent on the reciprocities of group life. Maslow's paragon of the "self-actualized" person ("authentic, individuated, productive," with "a surprising amount of detachment from people in general") begins to sound less like a social creature than a self-pollinating flower.

Taking potshots at Maslow may be a little unfair. At a time when psychology was obsessed with what goes wrong in the psyche, Maslow championed the things that go right. He was an exuberant advocate of human potential when most shrinks spent their fifty-minute hours chronicling pathology. And he did posit that self-actualization would inevitably lead to responsibility for others. But his emphasis on personal growth as the be-all helped spawn a national cottage industry devoted to building a better me, some enhanced self-to-the-tenth-power with its full entitlement of psychospiritual fabulousness. Not such an awful idea, I suppose, but as the song goes, is that all there is?

I dropped in on a human potential workshop recently. Plenty of talk about self-empowerment and self-realization, self-efficacy and peak performance, but compassion didn't rate a second billing on the marquee. It made me wonder what sort of selfhood we're seeking: the self that "gets its needs met" but is never fulfilled? Or the self that abundantly gives yet is never emptied? Instead of self-discovery, what about *other*-discovery, our real terra incognita?

I wonder too (as a pragmatic question, not a moral one) if this pedal-to-the-metal pursuit of happiness really does make us any happier, or if we have the whole thing backward. "The American way is to first feel good about yourself, and then feel good about others," notes the Benedictine monk Thomas Keating. "But spiritual traditions say it's the other way around—that you develop a sense of goodness by giving of yourself."

I have a few friends who embody the brand of beneficent love some researchers refer to as "generativity." I'd first gotten to know Alicia and Paul (not their real names) when I was teetering at the edge of a private cliff-hanger. They'd heard I was hurting, and though they barely knew me, they'd shown up one day with a check that pulled me back from the brink. No strings, they'd assured me as I stammered my thanks. I didn't have to do good with it, reciprocate in any way tangible or intangible, or even, they joked, have dinner with them. Just *be*, they said. It wasn't just the sum— several months' food and rent—that startled me, but the clear sense I got of the givers' unencumbered hearts.

Over the years, we've become close friends. Alicia and Paul live on a hilltop bordered by redwood forest with their three kids, a cockatoo, an ancient desert tortoise, a once-feral cat, a snake, and a pet white rat, all of whom gather around their large breakfast table each morning and seem to get along famously. The family is both well-off and deeply well-intentioned. They save swatches of rainforest; they build schools and teach in them; they take political refugees into their home; they plant community gardens, digging in the dirt. The last time I saw her, Alicia had just received her massage certification so she could give dying hospice patients the tenderness of her touch.

I sat in their kitchen one recent morning, looking out on a vista that was almost absurdly breathtaking: clement, mist-shrouded valleys undulating like bumps in a green carpet, rolling up to the edge of a silver sea. Paul wandered in for breakfast. Soon, so did a pet rooster, its spurs clicking regally over the ochre tiles until, abandoning all dignity, it leaped onto his lap. "It's spooky," he said. "Even our animals are nice." He wasn't bragging, just bemused. With his straw-blond hair and a ruddy, open face, Paul's surfer-dude placidity yields only occasional glimpses of the shrewd businessman who secured the family's fortunes. He clearly adores his kids, who are all stalwart, funny, and for tweeners, preternaturally considerate. He doesn't see himself as particularly compassionate, he tells me, just lucky—lucky to have made enough money to be able to give some away, lucky to have met his wife.

He credits Alicia for giving him the compassion 411: "Philanthropy's not that hard. Learning how to be kind to people—that's more elusive. Alicia's sort of a genius in that department."

I can attest to it. She makes you feel so favored—as if you'd done something extraordinary by simply existing—that you can't help but osmose a little of whatever she has and try to pass it along. Alicia, I'd always assumed, was one of those from-the-cradle lovebugs, born with some extra endowment of solar warmth.

"You've got to be kidding," she says. If anything, she insists, she was "born sad, not sweet," an anxious, self-enclosed kid. It was her mother, a "kind of saintly" woman with an eighth-grade education, who got through her shell. "She flat-out taught me compassion. She told me that life's greatest joy was to 'pull the beauty out of people,' because that makes your life beautiful too. She was rock solid in her devotion to other people. She'd be there for that superannoying person no one else wanted to be around, take care of the one who'd landed in the biggest mess. She adopted every single fuck-up in my family and a fair number of passing strangers." At age eighty-five, her mother still corresponds weekly with dozens of people in varying degrees of muddle and distress, people who, Alicia says, "count on her letters to help them hold on."

"I'm not at all like her," Alicia claims. "I'm much more critical of people. Mom kept saying the secret was just to take a genuine interest in others—just ask them questions, want to know how they are, really. I'd try that and it would feel good, so I'd do it some more. Step by step, I got to see how wonderful that sensation is of serving others." Alicia also credits her kids ("They taught me how to nurture—but that's nothing unusual, right?"), a few books, and sundry gurus. But she says it wasn't until she met Tommy that it all came together.

He had dropped by one day to visit a friend who was doing some construction on their house. Tommy had been told he had less than a year to live: AIDS. He had no money. No place to stay. "Well, it just seemed so obvious," says Alicia. "Not just to say, 'Gee, I'm so sorry, good luck'; but (*duh!*) 'You can stay *here*.'" Alicia and her family and a group of friends agreed to divide up the tasks. "I assigned myself to care for him physically, give him massages, that kind of thing. And I found I just loved it. When you see the suffering a person's enduring, there's no way you can't respond.

It takes you beyond yourself. Suddenly all those judgments you'd make if you just met them at a party evaporate. You're stripped down to two people doing their best to partake of this mystery."

Tommy had been walking with a cane when they first met him. Six months later, he was a quadriplegic. "But god," Alicia says, "was he fun! He had this sparkly, devilish, bad-boy quality. Even when he was really sick, he'd want to go down to Baja and throw some big soiree, so we'd organize this whole elaborate caravan of his friends and our friends and IVs and wheelchairs, and just *do* it. You think you've loved before, but this kind of thing opens your heart a thousand times. Tommy seemed to get more and more transparent the closer he got to death, and it enfolded you. I was with him when he died, when that transparency just turned into light."

Her weekly hospice work grew out of that experience. Alicia, at fifty, still has that lean, blonde, freckled, California-girl look, her shoulders tan and muscular from paddling in the surf. It's easy to imagine her large, strong hands kneading the failing flesh and comforting the moribund. But aren't there times, I press her, when you wonder why you're putting yourself through this; when you think of other things you could be doing—times you feel repulsed?

"I would have thought so," she says. "But the worse it got, somehow the more I felt attracted. After all the surgeries, the bodies look like battle-fields. You feel the loneliness of that person whose skin is falling off, who has tubes coming in and out of everywhere. And still, behind this war-torn shell, you feel the incredible strength of humanity. It may sound strange and corny, but there's nothing more heavenly than connecting with that."

Alicia's no sentimental pushover. She says she has a "fierce" side. She describes one of her charges who was "frankly an asshole, and the fact that he was dying hardly softened that one bit. He ticked me off something terrible. I had to draw the line: I'm not just a rug to be walked on, and I'm not doing you a favor if I let you." But she's learned to do something when she feels cornered, to "clear away evaluation and just rest someplace that doesn't have all those opinionated *voices* in it. When you do that, then out comes this love that melts people—not melts who they are, but who they *aren't*. Finding that is just like finding yourself. It makes you feel great." She laughs. "I swear, it's a totally *selfish* thing."

While we've been talking, the phone has been ringing. And ringing. Somebody wants something. Alicia gets up to answer. "If we can't help each other, what's the point?" she says. "Everything else gets kinda old after a while."

Now I'm not trying to sell you on Alicia and Paul as Mother Teresa and Mahatma Gandhi. They've had rough patches like any couple; they're spiritually unfancy folk. They enjoy their bounty with a contagious joie de vivre. You could quibble that, sure, it's easy to open your heart in the lap of luxury, but I've met insanely wealthy people who are more miserable than Midas.

Besides which, I know another family that's just like Alicia and Paul's, except they're living a gritty existence barely above the poverty line. If 90 percent of life is showing up, they go the other ten. Their door is always open, even if the weathered porch is sagging in. There's always a pot of chili on the stove. If you drop by, their easy affection embraces you (and you, and you too). Their small living room feels crowded with conviviality. You can stay a few nights on the fraying couch if cat dander and dog hair don't bother you too much. They take care of jobs and kids and ailing grandparents and friends' troubles and community causes, and when I ask them how they do it, they say, "Do what?"

Folks like these have basically eliminated any option of pretending I don't know what we can be for each other. I know for a fact I could stand to be kinder, more generous, fiercer in cleaving to the good, true, and beautiful. It could be worth a shot. I've been pondering something John of the Cross wrote: "Where you find no love, put love, and you will find love." Maybe he had some idea what he was talking about.

One evening, I gathered a random assemblage of people to chew the fat about love. Heady types mostly, some with sharp elbows, so they were a little cautious at first. "There's no remedy for love," said a poet, lamenting its "misconception and intrigue." But after they'd proved to each other they weren't soppy romantics, they admitted there was more to the story.

"Love dismantles the whole judgment thing," said one, a lawyer. "The sluice gates open, and more water flows over the dam. When that happens, *love*'s a verb—you can love anything."

"When we're in love, we're a love *factory*," a woman said. "We're churning out so much, we have tons extra to give away."

"Whenever you love," opined a political activist, "you're undermining consumer culture. Who needs all that *stuff* when you have other people?" He gave a little smirk. "Like they say, accept no substitutes!"

"Love is like the great, pulsating orb in old sci-fi movies," someone effused toward the end of an increasingly well-oiled evening. "The one where no matter how many missiles you fire at it, it just absorbs them all and keeps getting bigger and bigger!"

After they tumbled out into the night, noticeably buoyed, I thought about that last one. *Doesn't* love encompass everything you can throw at it? Doesn't the whole human repertoire spiral out of and circle back to love? Even justice, Martin Luther King Jr., once said, is only "love correcting that which revolts against love." It may have been the evening's wine talking, but suddenly everything seemed to have *something* to do with love. The same love molecule, like water, everywhere, in every form: boiling into steam as passion, or freezing into glistening hate, or just flowing upstream and downstream, into every crack and crevice, irreducible.

Don't know how to maneuver with your husband, wife, boyfriend, girlfriend, boss, employee, parent, child, friend, enemy? Love! Everything else is just a finger in the dike, holding back an ocean that, ironically, you could happily drown in. Sometimes I think, trying to get it through my own thick seawall of a skull, that compassion means only this: When in doubt, *just love.*

By the next morning, the effects of the evening's mild bacchanal had worn off, but I still half-believed it.

My Vows

Susan Piver

To love all beings, to love even one—author and meditation instructor Susan Piver decides to commit.

So far, I've made two vows that have changed my life. One was related to my Buddhist practice—to become a bodhisattva. The other was to become a wife.

A bodhisattva is a person who vows to help all beings reach enlightenment, no matter how many lifetimes it might take. This vow is obviously not made lightly; it comes after many hours of meditation practice and a formal commitment to Buddhism. Serious contemplation and study are required to get even a glimmer of the deeper meaning of this vow and its complexities. (For example, you vow to love everyone, even people you don't like.)

A wife's vow is also not made lightly. It comes after having found someone you really, really like to talk to and also to touch. It's made after serious contemplation of the likelihood you'll find anyone better, might otherwise grow old alone, and how cute you'd look in a bridal gown. A bodhisattva chooses to be of service. A bride picks out china patterns for dinner service.

It so happened that I prepared to take both these vows at around the same time. While bride-me was shopping for dresses, arguing with her parents, and falling prey to panic attacks, bodhisattva-me was contemplating the suffering of all sentient beings.

Both are vows to love (all beings in one case and a single being in the other), and it may seem that the bodhisattva vow is the really hard one. But after ten years, I can tell you that the real test of bigheartedness started with the latter proposition.

When my boyfriend asked me to marry him, I didn't exactly gush yes. I sort of tried to break up with him. He wanted to deepen our relationship, and I just wasn't sure. I loved Duncan, but my divorced girlfriends had loved their boyfriends too. Clearly love was no basis for marriage. Then what was? It had to be about more than wearing a silly dress, waving a wedding ring around, and being all "Oh, it's my day."

I told him I needed time to think it over and wanted to spend a month apart. I planned to search my soul, ponder the question deeply, and meditate *a lot*. I didn't really know if I was cut out for marriage. I prized my solitude tremendously, maybe above everything. When I wanted to write, I wrote. When I wanted to meditate, I meditated. When I wanted to pretend to write and meditate, no one was around to bust me. I wasn't sure I wanted to give all this up.

Plus, right now we could easily ignore what drove each of us crazy about the other, and perhaps as a consequence, after five years we were still completely hot for each other. Privacy. Being able to get away from each other on our bad days. These were good things, no? Maybe maintaining some separation was the key to keeping the whole thing going.

By month's end, I figured I'd either have come to some sort of brilliant conclusion about how it could all work out *or* realize I simply wasn't built for marriage and we should break up. If the latter, I'd already have accumulated separation days, and maybe they could be backdated to shorten the grieving period.

During all this, I noticed that I was crying a lot. Everything was touching me, and it was getting on my nerves: the hopeful look on a colleague's face when he was about to make a presentation, how sorry I felt for the people on the news, how beautiful Marvin Gaye's voice was when he sang "What's Going On." The insulation between me and the world around me was getting thinner and thinner. So I stepped up my meditation practice. I thought this would be the best way to maintain equilibrium during this emotional time. But the more I meditated, the more likely I was to be provoked to tears by the slightest display of fragility. This couldn't be the in-tended result. Instead of making me peaceful, meditating was freaking me out. What was I doing wrong?

I made an appointment with my meditation instructor to explore this question, but instead of giving me a strategy for toughening up, he suggested I take the bodhisattva vow. He explained that *bodhi* meant "awake" and *sattva* meant "being," so an awakened being is what you vow to become.

He told me that the vow was something a Buddhist might consider to deepen her practice after having been a meditator for some years. (Again with the deepening.) *Sure,* I thought, *who wouldn't want to try to become enlightened?* But there was a catch. "The vow is to attain enlightenment for all beings, not just for yourself. You vow to keep taking birth through endless lifetimes and helping out until *all beings* are enlightened," he said. No exceptions. You volunteer to take on the pain of all others. *Wow, that's some vow,* I thought. "But how," I asked him, "will this help me stop crying all the time?" It sounded like it would make everything worse. "The tears are a good sign," he said. "It's good preparation for the path of the bodhisattva." *Okay, if you say so,* I thought to myself.

I spent a month weighing the pros and cons of getting married, figuring that at some point one would outweigh the other. One problem with my strategy: the more I thought it all over, the more I realized that I totally, completely loved this person Duncan, and there was nothing I could do about it. No matter how heavy the con side of the list got with perfectly acceptable reasons not to marry (familiarity kills desire, all my private time will disappear, I can't poop when anyone else is in the house), it couldn't trump the one solitary thing on the pro side: I loved him. (Okay, and there would be tax advantages.) I didn't even know *why* I loved him so much. I mean, he's great and cute and funny and all that, but nothing could account for the pleasure I got from his breath on my shoulder as we fell asleep or how upsetting I found it when anyone was mean to him.

When we got back together after our month apart, I told him how much I loved him and gave him a carefully thought-out list of caveats: I'd never be a conventional wife. I'd require time and space to meditate every day. Please don't talk to me when I'm in the bathroom. And so on. In the midst of my big presentation, he reached into his backpack and retrieved a small package. *Oh no,* I thought. *Does he think that giving me a ring will wash away all doubts and common sense?*

But there was no ring. Instead, he handed me a little heart-shaped box. Inside was a backyard bird feather and a smooth white stone. "This is us," he said. "I'm the rock, and you're the feather. Fly all you want. That's just who you are. I'll make our situation stable. That's who I am." I was flabbergasted. What? He saw me this clearly and still wanted to marry me? The gravity of my rules and conditions shifted as suddenly as a flock of birds in the sky. My heart simply melted, and I burst into tears. I had no idea there could be a person as wonderful as him. At this point, there was no choice. "Yes," I said. "Yes, yes, yes. Please marry me, and I will marry you."

So we began to plan our wedding. I placed the sweet box with the rock and the feather by my bed so I could look at it anytime I wanted. Whenever we would have a fight or my doubts would return, I could lift the top and peek inside. *Oh yes,* I would remind myself, *everything is okay. We love each other so much.*

Also during this month, I was studying in preparation for the bodhisattva vow ceremony. I read about how great saints and scholars defined compassion and how they kept it going even under the most difficult circumstances. I learned that compassion is the sole basis for peace and that personal happiness can only come from making the needs of others primary. I once read that the Dalai Lama spends three hours every morning rousing compassion. How did he then go out into the world without sobbing all the time? I had no idea. But just as with marrying Duncan, after thinking it over, I realized that I had to do it. There was simply no choice. Do you say no when the one you love offers to love you back for the rest of his life? Do you say no when your meditation teacher asks if you want to try to become enlightened for the benefit of others? "Actually, I think I'd rather remain in a self-absorbed fantasy" didn't seem like a good answer to either of them. So I said yes. Okay, yes, yes, yes. I'll try.

Within a few months, I took the bodhisattva vow with about ten other students. We had been told to bring something to place on the altar as an offering during the ceremony. It didn't have to be the most meaningful thing in our life, but it should be something that mattered. I thought about offering a ring my mother had given me that I rarely wore or books that had been very meaningful to me or even my favorite dress. (Look, I really loved that dress.) None of them seemed right. There was only one thing that would cost me to be without: the box with the rock and the feather. I tried to talk myself out it: "He said it didn't have to be our most valued possession. That would hurt Duncan. Surely I could hold on to this."

I didn't know if I was making a generous gesture or a martyry one when I offered the box during the vow ceremony. But I did it anyway.

The very next morning, I woke up in a panic. I was bereft. I wanted that box back. I had never possessed anything so precious. But it was gone, and nothing, nothing, nothing could bring it back. Even if I could find it and return it to my bedside table, it would now only be a sad reminder of how selfish I was, not how beloved. I was stuck. I saw just how unlikely a candidate for bodhisattvahood I was. I couldn't even graciously give up a cardboard box for the benefit of others, to say nothing of my "personal space" for my boyfriend. Could I change my mind about these vows, or was it too late?

Too late. I had already gotten my first lesson. You can't give to get. Opening yourself to another isn't as simple as acting nice or giving up what you value even though you really, really don't want to. It's actually heartbreaking. I started to cry for the zillionth time since I had been contemplating all these vows. I knew I had no idea how to be a bodhisattva— or a wife, for that matter. Nor could I pretend these were stupid ideas and go back to living the way I had before. Anything I gained for myself alone would be a reminder of my lack of loving-kindness. I couldn't be bodhisattva Susan, but I couldn't be regular Susan either. Bastards! I was trapped. So, of course, I burst into tears.

Instead of making it safe, love—whether for all beings or for one— actually breaks your heart. Being loved is uncomfortable and the more I love, the more uncomfortable it is. In the end, I'm still not quite sure what I've vowed to do either as a wife or as a bodhisattva, except to break my own heart, over and over, and see what happens next.

Contributors

Marc Ian Barasch is an award-winning writer, editor, songwriter, and television producer. He has been editor in chief of *New Age Journal,* a contributing editor at *Psychology Today,* and editor at large for *Natural Health.* He has been short-listed twice for the PEN Award and is the author of a number of books, including *The Compassionate Life: Walking the Path of Kindness.*

Ezra Bayda has been practicing meditation since 1970 and received dharma transmission in 1998. He lives, writes, and teaches at Zen Center San Diego. His latest book is *Beyond Happiness: The Zen Way to True Contentment.*

Richard Borofsky, along with his wife, Antra, is the cofounder and codirector of the Center for the Study of Relationship in Cambridge, Massachusetts, which provides therapy and workshops for couples and individuals on the practice of relationship. He is a contributor to *On Intimate Ground: A Gestalt Approach to Working with Couples* and read love poems on the CD *Joyful Wedding: A Spiritual Path to the Altar.*

Tara Brach, PhD, the author of *Radical Acceptance,* is a clinical psychologist as well as a Buddhist lay priest and popular teacher of mindfulness meditation. She is the founder of the Insight Meditation Community in Washington, D.C., and has conducted workshops at Spirit Rock Center, Omega Institute, the New York Open Center, and other retreat centers nationwide.

GABRIEL COHEN is the author of five novels and a nonfiction book called *Storms Can't Hurt the Sky: A Buddhist Path through Divorce*. He has also written for the *New York Times, Lion's Roar, Poets & Writers,* and other publications. He lectures and conducts workshops frequently and teaches at the Pratt Institute.

The Fourteenth Dalai Lama, TENZIN GYATSO, is the spiritual and temporal leader of the Tibetan people and a winner of the Nobel Peace Prize. He is also a profound Buddhist teacher who is the author or coauthor of many best-selling books, including *Worlds in Harmony: Compassionate Action for a Better World* and *The Art of Happiness: A Handbook for Living*.

NORMAN FISCHER is the founder of the Everyday Zen Foundation, whose mission is to open and broaden Zen practice through what he calls "engaged renunciation." Fischer practiced and taught at the San Francisco Zen Center for twenty-five years and served as abbot from 1995 until 2000. He is the author of *Sailing Home: The Spiritual Journey as an Odyssey of Return*.

JOSEPH GOLDSTEIN is a guiding teacher and cofounder of the Insight Meditation Society in Barre, Massachusetts. He lectures and leads retreats around the world and is author of *One Dharma: The Emerging Western Buddhism, The Experience of Insight,* and *A Heart Full of Peace*. Goldstein first became interested in Buddhism as a Peace Corps volunteer in Thailand in 1965.

ELLEN GRAF is a writer and sculptor in rural upstate New York, where she lives with her husband, Lu Zhong-hua. She is the author of *The Natural Laws of Good Luck: A Memoir of an Unlikely Marriage,* which was selected for Barnes and Noble's Discover New Authors promotion and Borders' Original Voices program; it was also an Indie Next List Notable pick.

JANE HAMILTON is a best-selling novelist who lives in Wisconsin. She is the author of *The Book of Ruth,* winner of the PEN/Hemingway Award for first fiction, and *A Map of the World,* a *New York Times* Notable Book of the Year. Both *The Book of Ruth* and *A Map of the World* have been selections of Oprah's Book Club. Her most recent novel is *Laura Rider's Masterpiece*.

THICH NHAT HANH (1926–2022) was a global spiritual leader, poet, and peace activist. He authored more than forty books, including *Peace Is Every Step: The Path of Mindfulness in Everyday Life* and *True Love: A Practice for Awakening the Heart.*

ERIK HANSEN teaches screenwriting at the University of New Orleans. His screen credits include the feature film *Heart and Souls,* starring Robert Downey Jr.; a Student Academy Award–winning short film; and the recently completed *The Princess Wife.* His writing has appeared in two volumes of *The Best Buddhist Writing.*

MOH HARDIN is an *acharya,* or senior teacher, in the Shambhala Buddhist lineage. The son of a Methodist minister, he graduated from Duke University with a BA in music. He lives in Halifax, Nova Scotia, and teaches Buddhism and meditation in Canada and the United States. He is the author of *A Little Book of Love: Practical Advice on Bringing Happiness and Peace to Our World.*

ARTHUR JEON has an MFA from the University of Southern California's film school, and he lived in Los Angeles and worked in the film industry as a screenwriter for ten years. He currently teaches yoga at Yoga Works in Santa Monica, California. He is the author of *City Dharma: Keeping Your Cool in the Chaos* and *Sex, Love, and Dharma: Finding Love without Losing Your Way.*

JAMES KULLANDER, MDIV, is a program curriculum developer for Omega Institute in Rhinebeck, New York, and a consultant for online course development. He also leads meditation and writing retreats. His work has been published in a variety of publications, including the *Sun, Lion's Roar,* the *New York Times,* and on Beliefnet.com.

RABBI HAROLD KUSHNER, PHD, was born in Brooklyn, New York, and graduated from Columbia University. Best known as the author of *When Bad Things Happen to Good People,* an international bestseller first published in 1981, he also wrote *When All You've Ever Wanted Isn't Enough,* which was awarded the Christopher Medal for its contribution to the exaltation of the human spirit.

GERI LARKIN was ordained on July 2, 1995, following her training in the Maitreya Buddhist Seminary. She is the founding teacher of Still Point Zen Buddhist Temple located in Detroit and the author of various books, including *Love Dharma, Chocolate Cake Sutra,* and *Plant Seed, Pull Weed.*

JENNIFER LAUCK has written three memoirs and a collection of essays, including the *New York Times* bestseller *Blackbird* and *Found,* released by Seal Press. She has her MFA in creative writing from Pacific Lutheran University and was an award-winning investigative TV reporter. Lauck has studied Tibetan Buddhism for nearly ten years, is a dedicated meditation student, and has received teachings from many great masters including the Fourteenth Dalai Lama, Adzom Rinpoche, and eco-philosopher Joanna Macy.

KAREN MAEZEN MILLER, a priest at the Hazy Moon Zen Center in Los Angeles, is the author of *Momma Zen* and *Hand Wash Cold: Care Instructions for an Ordinary Life.* You can keep up with her through her blog, *Cheerio Road.* She lives with husband and daughter in Sierra Madre, California.

BARRY MAGID is a psychiatrist and psychoanalyst in New York City. He established the Ordinary Mind Zendo as an affiliate of the San Diego Zen Center and serves as its Zen teacher. He is the author of *Ordinary Mind: Exploring the Common Ground of Zen and Psychoanalysis* and *Ending the Pursuit of Happiness: A Zen Guide.*

LAURA MUNSON is a writer who lives in Whitefish, Montana. She is the author of the memoir *This Is Not the Story You Think It Is: A Season of Unlikely Happiness.* Her short stories and essays have appeared in various literary journals and magazines.

SUSAN PIVER, author, meditation teacher, and graduate of Buddhist seminary, is a frequent guest on network television, including *The Oprah Winfrey Show, Today,* and *The Tyra Banks Show.* Her best-selling books include *The Hard Questions: 100 Questions to Ask before You Say "I Do"* and *The Wisdom of a Broken Heart: An Uncommon Guide to Healing, Insight, and Love.*

DZOGCHEN PONLOP is a meditation master and scholar in the Kagyu and Nyingma schools of Tibetan Buddhism. He is the president of Nalandabodhi, a network of meditation centers, and founder of the Nitartha Institute, a course of Buddhist study for Western students. He is also the author of *Rebel Buddha, Wild Awakening,* and *Mind beyond Death.*

DAVID RICHO, PHD, MFT, is a psychotherapist and teacher in Santa Barbara and San Francisco, California, who emphasizes Jungian, transpersonal, and spiritual perspectives in his work. His books include *How to Be an Adult in Relationships, Daring to Trust,* and *The Five Things We Cannot Change.*

BRENDA SHOSHANNA, a psychologist and practitioner of both Zen and Judaism, is the author of several books, including *Fearless: The 7 Principles of Peace of Mind* and *Zen and the Art of Falling in Love.* Her work focuses on integrating East and West, and she offers workshops on relationships and personal and spiritual development.

JUDITH SIMMER-BROWN leads workshops across North America on how meditation can help us create more fulfilling and lasting intimate relationships. She has been a core faculty member in religious studies at Naropa University since 1978, and she is the author of *Dakini's Warm Breath: The Feminine Principle in Tibetan Buddhism.*

KAREN KISSEL WEGELA, PHD, has been studying and teaching the integration of Buddhist principles and psychotherapy for three decades. She is a professor of contemplative psychotherapy at Naropa University and the author of *The Courage to Be Present: Buddhism, Psychotherapy, and the Awakening of Natural Wisdom.*

JOHN WELWOOD, PHD (1943–2019), was a psychologist and student of Tibetan Buddhism for more than thirty-five years. He led workshops on the integration of psychological and spiritual work nationally and internationally. His books include *Journey of the Heart, Toward a Psychology of Awakening,* and *Perfect Love, Imperfect Relationships.*

DIANA WINSTON, the director of mindfulness education at UCLA's Mindful Awareness Research Center, brings a gentle, secular approach to teaching mindfulness across the age spectrum. She has brought mindful awareness into schools, hospitals, and nonprofits, as well as to adolescents, seniors, teachers, activists, and health professionals. The author of *Wide Awake: A Buddhist Guide for Teens,* she's a former Buddhist nun and a teacher at Spirit Rock Meditation Center.

POLLY YOUNG-EISENDRATH, PhD, a Jungian psychoanalyst, is clinical associate professor of psychiatry and clinical associate professor of psychology at the University of Vermont and clinical supervisor and consultant on leadership development at Norwich University. A longtime Buddhist practitioner, she is the author of more than a dozen books, including *You're Not What I Expected: Love after the Romance Has Ended.*

Credits

PART 1: VISIONS OF MINDFUL LOVING

Thich Nhat Hanh, "Love Is Being Present." From *True Love: A Practice for Awakening the Heart* by Thich Nhat Hanh. © 2004 by the Unified Buddhist Church, Inc. Reprinted by arrangement with Shambhala Publications, Inc., Boulder, CO, www.shambhala.com.

Diana Winston, "Saying Yes to an Open Heart." From the Summer 2010 issue of *Buddhadharma*.

Dzogchen Ponlop, "The Great Mirror of Relationship." From the November 2009 issue of the *Shambhala Sun* (now *Lion's Roar*).

Judith Simmer-Brown, "Going Beyond Disappointment." From the November 2009 issue of the *Shambhala Sun* (now *Lion's Roar*).

Norman Fischer, "Falling in Love." From the July 1999 issue of the *Shambhala Sun* (now *Lion's Roar*).

PART 2: PREPARING THE GROUND

Moh Hardin, "Making Friends with Ourselves." From *A Little Book of Love: Practical Advice on Bringing Happiness to Ourselves and Our World* by Moh Hardin. © 2011 by Moh Hardin. Reprinted by arrangement with Shambhala Publications, Inc., Boulder, CO, www.shambhala.com.

Part 3: Being in Relationship

Ellen Graf, "Memoir of an Unlikely Marriage." From *The Natural Laws of Good Luck* by Ellen Graf. © 2009 by Ellen Graf. Reprinted by arrangement with Shambhala Publications, Inc., Boulder, CO, www.shambhala.com.

Arthur Jeon, "Present Moment Listening." From *Sex, Love, and Dharma: Finding Love Without Losing Your Way* by Arthur Jeon. Copyright © 2005 by Arthur Jeon. Published by Three Rivers Press. Reprinted by agreement with the author.

PART 4: DEALING WITH DIFFICULTIES

Laura Munson, "Those Aren't Fighting Words, Dear." From the *New York Times,* July 31. © 2009 the *New York Times* All rights reserved. Used by permission and protected by the Copyright Laws of the United States. The printing, copying, redistribution, or retransmission of the Material without express written permission is prohibited.

Brenda Shoshanna, "It Used to Be So Exciting." Adapted with the permission of Simon & Schuster, Inc., from *Zen and the Art of Falling in Love* by Brenda Shoshanna. Copyright © 2003 by Brenda Shoshanna. All rights reserved.

Polly Young-Eisendrath, "The Hidden Treasure of Anger." From the March 2010 issue of the *Shambhala Sun* (now *Lion's Roar*).

Geri Larkin, "The Green-Eyed Monster." From *Love Dharma: Relationship Wisdom from Enlightened Buddhist Women* by Geri Larkin. Copyright © 2002 by Geri Larkin. Reprinted with permission of Tuttle Publishing, www.tuttlepublishing.com.

James Kullander, "My Marital Status." From the December 2007 issue of *The Sun.*

PART 5: GROWING APART

Susan Piver, "Making Friends with Heartbreak." Reprinted with permission of Free Press, a Division of Simon & Schuster, Inc., from *The Wisdom of a*

Gabriel Cohen, "Of Course I'm Angry." From the September 2008 issue of the *Shambhala Sun* (now *Lion's Roar*).

Karen Kissel Wegela, "I Think We Should Stop Seeing Each Other." From the July 1999 issue of *Shambhala Sun* (now *Lion's Roar*).

David Richo, "When Relationships End." From *How to Be an Adult in Relationships* by David Richo. © 2002 by David Richo. Reprinted by arrangement with Shambhala Publications, Inc., Boulder, CO, www.shambhala.com.

Jennifer Lauck, "Let It Bee." Previously unpublished. Published by arrangement with the author.

PART 6: LOVE AS SPIRITUAL PRACTICE

John Welwood, "Intimate Relationship as a Spiritual Crucible." From the November 2008 issue of the *Shambhala Sun* (now *Lion's Roar*).

Richard Borofsky, "Marriage as a Path of Compassion." From the September/November 2001 issue of *Mandala*.

Joseph Goldstein, "May All Beings Be Happy." Adapted from *A Heart Full of Peace* by Joseph Goldstein. Copyright © 2007 by Joseph Goldstein. Used by permission of Wisdom Publications.

The Fourteenth Dalai Lama, "That's the Power of Love." From *Live in a Better Way* and *The Transformed Mind,* edited by Renuka Singh. Copyright © 1999 by His Holiness the Dalai Lama. Used by permission of Viking Penguin, a division of Penguin Group (USA) Inc. Also reproduced by permission of Hodder and Stoughton Limited.

Marc Ian Barasch, "Searching for the Heart of Compassion." Adapted from *Field Notes on the Compassionate Life: A Search for the Soul of Kindness* by Marc Ian Barasch. Copyright © 2005 by Marc Ian Barasch, published by Rodale Books. Reprinted by agreement with the author.

Susan Piver, "My Vows." From the July 2008 issue of the *Shambhala Sun* (now *Lion's Roar*).

About Lion's Roar

Lion's Roar is an independent nonprofit whose mission is to communicate Buddhist wisdom and practice in order to benefit people's lives and society, and to support the development of Buddhism in the modern world—presenting the breadth and depth of the full diversity of Buddhist lineages.

Lion's Roar magazine is the largest circulation Buddhist publication in the English language. Many video and audio offerings, live events, and more are also featured on lionsroar.com, with dedicated sections on Buddhadharma (supporting committed Buddhist practitioners), El Camino del Buda (featuring Buddhist teachings in Spanish), and Bodhi Leaves (celebrating Buddhists of Asian descent). By bringing Buddhist wisdom to bear on current events and perennial human concerns, the work of Lion's Roar helps to point the way toward a society that prizes, cultivates, and can uphold universal values like compassion, generosity, wisdom, and peace.